We Love you!
Happy Birthday!
Grandma Vickie & Carlos

We Love you!
Happy Birthday!
Grandma Vickie & Carlos

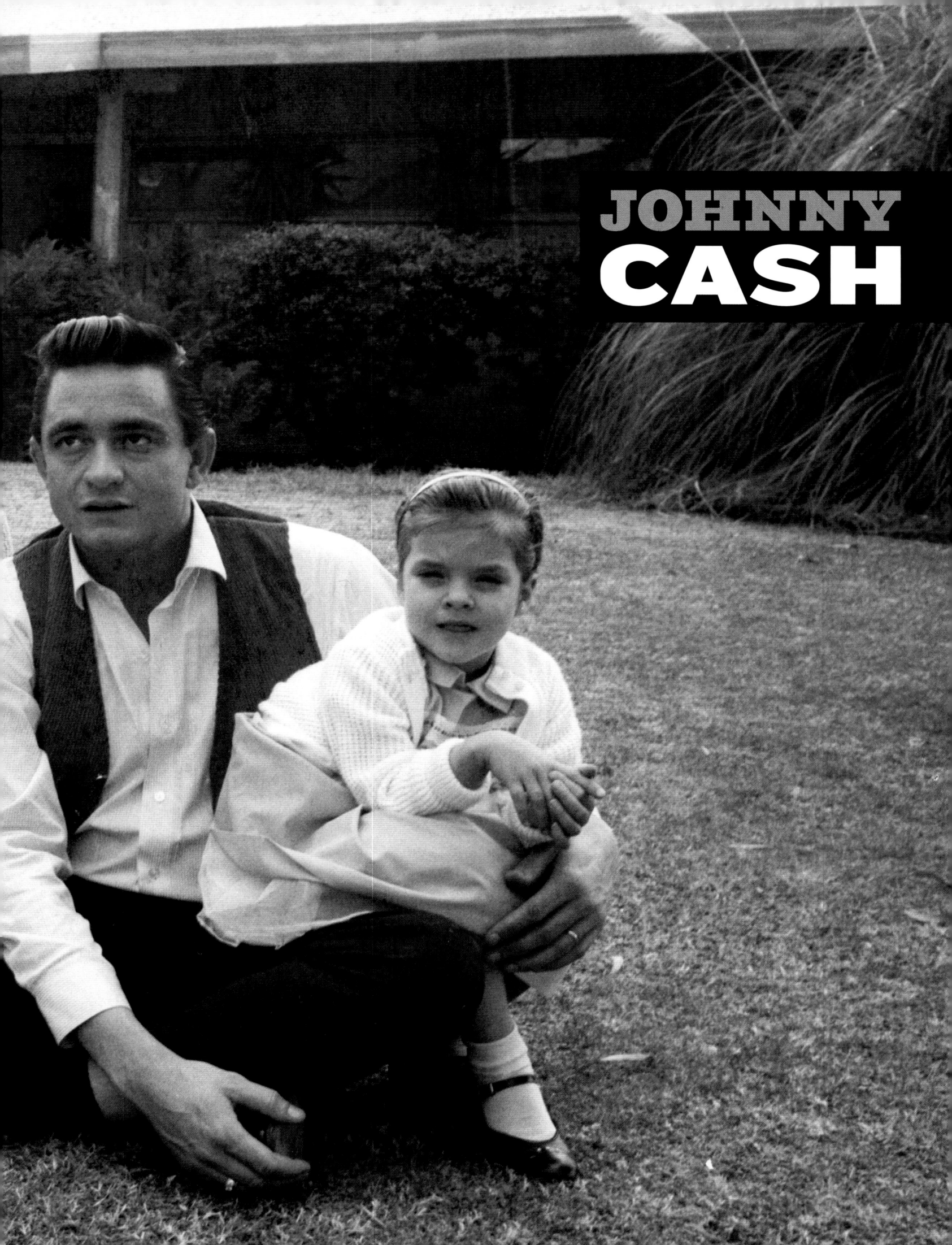

JOHNNY CASH

LIFE BOOKS

Managing Editor
Robert Sullivan

Director of Photography
Barbara Baker Burrows

Creative Direction
Li'l Robin Design, Inc.

Deputy Picture Editor
Christina Lieberman

Writer-Reporters
Michelle DuPré,
Daniel S. Levy

Copy Chief
Parlan McGaw

Copy Editor
Barbara Gogan

Photo Associate
Sarah Cates

Consulting Picture Editors
Mimi Murphy (Rome),
Tala Skari (Paris)

Special thanks: Rosanne Cash, John
Carter Cash, Danny Kahn, Lou Robin,
Tom Tierney, Ché Williams

Editorial Director
Stephen Koepp

EDITORIAL OPERATIONS

Richard K. Prue (Director), Brian
Fellows (Manager), Richard Shaffer
(Production), Keith Aurelio, Charlotte
Coco, Liz Grover, Kevin Hart, Mert
Kerimoglu, Rosalie Khan, Patricia
Koh, Marco Lau, Brian Mai, Po Fung
Ng, Rudi Papiri, Robert Pizaro,
Barry Pribula, Clara Renauro, Katy
Saunders, Hia Tan, Vaune Trachtman

TIME HOME ENTERTAINMENT

President
Jim Childs

Vice President, Brand & Digital Strategy
Steven Sandonato

Executive Director, Marketing Services
Carol Pittard

Executive Director, Retail & Special Sales
Tom Mifsud

Executive Publishing Director
Joy Butts

**Director, Bookazine Development
& Marketing** Laura Adam

Finance Director
Glenn Buonocore

Associate Publishing Director
Megan Pearlman

Assistant General Counsel
Helen Wan

Assistant Director, Special Sales
Ilene Schreider

Senior Book Production Manager
Susan Chodakiewicz

Design & Prepress Manager
Anne-Michelle Gallero

Brand Manager
Roshni Patel

Associate Prepress Manager
Alex Voznesenskiy

Assistant Brand Manager
Stephanie Braga

Special thanks: Katherine Barnet,
Jeremy Biloon, Rose Cirrincione,
Jacqueline Fitzgerald, Christine
Font, Jenna Goldberg, Hillary Hirsch,
David Kahn, Amy Mangus, Kimberly
Marshall, Amy Migliaccio, Nina Mistry,
Dave Rozzelle, Ricardo Santiago,
Adriana Tierno, Vanessa Wu

Page 1: With his Gibson in 1958.
PHOTOGRAPH BY JOHN HAMILTON

Pages 2–3: At home in California
with Vivian and their girls in 1960.
PHOTOGRAPH BY DON HUNSTEIN

These pages: At the Newport Folk
Festival in July 1964.
PHOTOGRAPH BY DAVID GAHR/GETTY

JOHNNY CASH

OPENING THE
TREASURE CHEST

Ten years ago, one of American music's greatest-ever families lost, within months, its two most famous members when Valerie June Carter Cash died at age 73 on May 15, 2003, followed on September 12 by her husband, John, who was 71. After the mourning, the family house was sold and many personal effects were stored or claimed by the children: musical instruments, unfinished songs, unknown recordings, photographs and memories. In the intervening decade, bits and pieces of this have seen the light of day, and "new" Johnny Cash music has been released. Much of it is wonderful; certainly we here at LIFE, who had been in touch with both John and June through the years for stories we were working on, enjoyed hearing it. We were pleased that the record labels with which Johnny Cash had been affiliated were finding this material, cleaning it up and sharing it with the world.

Principal among those labels was Sony Music Entertainment, which in 1988 acquired Columbia Records, John's home base for the bulk of his career. We were talking with our friends at Sony one day and a suggestion was made: "You folks really ought to see our photo archives. We've got thousands of pictures—Barbra Streisand, Tony Bennett, all sorts of folks who were and are on our labels, including Columbia. We've got Johnny Cash."

If we were excited when we heard that, we grew more so when we visited the quiet room in midtown Manhattan and began going through the meticulously catalogued files. Here was John with the children, here were the family reunions and weddings. Here were the behind-the-scenes shots from the prison concerts and studio sessions. Here were the outtakes from the photo shoots for album covers. Here was the house in California, and a wealth of color photography from the legendary lake house in Hendersonville, Tennessee. The phrase *treasure trove* is overused. But this was the very definition of a treasure trove.

We continued to talk with our friends at Sony, and a new line of LIFE books was imagined—the first of which you hold in your hands. LIFE Unseen will present some of the world's biggest stars as you've never known them. Choosing from among the best never-seen or rarely seen pictures— many of them intimate photographs made in quiet moments but which served no commercial purpose at the time—we will assemble illustrated biographies that are indispensable additions to any fan's library. You may own other Johnny

GUY GILLETTE

Cash books, but you don't have this one—until now.

Almost as soon as LIFE's editors started sifting through the Sony archive, we realized that we had to go further to produce something that wasn't simply a scrapbook but was, in fact, truly special: the whole big picture. Sony owned copies of some images you certainly do know: the famous silhouette shot from the cover of the classic *At San Quentin* album, for instance. We knew we needed to include such photography, and the Million Dollar Quartet picture from Sun Studio in Memphis, to keep the story flowing. There were clues in the archive: credit lines of talented photographers known to us for decades. And so, for instance, we approached the folks at Jim Marshall Photography, and sure enough, they found the John and Bob Dylan shot that we knew had to exist somewhere. We went to the House of Cash and obtained some of the

family's material; and to fill out the early, pre-Columbia years, we found a collection at Arkansas State University. So, yes: There is material here that has been published before. But even so, most of what you encounter will be new to you—fresh and alive.

How can we be so confident of that? Because we had one more idea: Let's show all of this to John's eldest child, the acclaimed singer-songwriter Rosanne Cash, and John and June's son, the award-winning musician and producer John Carter Cash, and see what they think. Let's ask if they were surprised or moved. What good times or painful times were rekindled by these pictures from the vault? We had a fine conversation with Rosanne on a Saturday morning in spring, and we're sure of two things: You will enjoy her reminiscences, which begin on the page immediately following; and you're going to be surprised by these pictures.

MOMENTS LIKE THIS, from 1958, fill these pages. In the background: the young girls; the boy who digs the guitarist.

If *she* was, how can you not be? And John Carter sent along his memories as well, which appear in places throughout the book. He also helped us sort out the cast of characters at the "guitar pull" on pages 116–117. Roy! Kris! *Jack Palance!*

The folks at Sony clearly got us thinking actively, and apparently we got them thinking as well. The publication of this first LIFE Unseen book coincides with their release of a new album, *Unheard Johnny Cash:* yet more discoveries and rarities from a music archive that is, if anything, even richer than this photographic record. "Photographic record" sounds prosaic. Call it, instead, a treasure trove—a treasure trove that, until now, was carefully kept under wraps in New York City. We're glad we found it. We think you will be, too.

ROSANNE CASH

John's first child, with Vivian Liberto Cash, was Rosanne, born in 1955 in Memphis, right around when her father was recording his very first tracks there for Sun Records. As we've already mentioned, John and June, Rosanne's stepmother, both died 10 years ago, and Vivian died in 2005. Rosanne is, therefore, the one still with us who was there for most all of what you will see in the pages to follow.

For more than three decades Rosanne herself has been in the highest echelon of American singer-songwriters, and in recent years has won acclaim for her fiction and nonfiction writing as well. Certainly on her last two terrific albums, *Black Cadillac* and *The List,* she has revisited her family's legacy, and thought back to the times they shared. Who better, then, to travel through these photographs? Rosanne lives in New York City today, and on a Saturday morning in the spring of 2013, she shares her thoughts after poring over these pages. As she talks, she dives deeper.

"I looked through all of the photographs and they're really wonderful," she begins. "I thought that there were some surprising choices, things that were really unexpected." She isn't entirely familiar with the earliest material from the collection out at Arkansas State: "My grandmother and grandfather on the porch, and the photos of my dad in the Air Force: It's really comprehensive, and I was really happy to see those included. And once he started singing professionally, the pictures of fans. One picture I really love is the one of him and Luther [Perkins] and this huge crowd of people in the background. That's fantastic." Perkins was Johnny Cash's guitarist from the very beginning—1954— until Perkins's death in 1968; the picture Rosanne refers to is on pages 36 and 37, and was taken as stardom was first happening for her father. The photograph kindles other memories: "Luther and Marshall [Grant, the bassist in the Memphis act that evolved into "Johnny Cash"] were always around. Marshall was always a lot closer to my family because Marshall's wife and my mom were best friends. But Luther was always around, too, and his wife—and it was devastating for everyone when Luther died. The band was always there, they were always there. It was absolutely like family.

"There's one when Dad's signing outside the bus, and Marshall's looking at what's going on." She is talking here of the photograph on pages 172 and 173. "That's a

microcosm of a few decades right there, Marshall taking care of everything, *everything.* I loved Marshall. I looked at that picture and thought about them all meeting. My dad's brother Roy worked at the Chrysler dealership, and Luther and Marshall were mechanics, and Roy came in and said, 'My brother's coming back from the Air Force and he could meet you. He plays guitar.' And my dad walks into the bay where they were working and Marshall looks up and the hair on his back stands up when he sees my dad. He knew that the rest of his life was bound up with this man."

There are pictures of other friends and collaborators, from later in the career. "Kris and Willie and Waylon," Rosanne says with a smile. "Dad was really, really close to Waylon and Kris particularly. Willie was a friend, but Waylon and Dad were always over at each other's house. Waylon—he was a sweetheart. He had his demons, but he was a sweetheart. And Kris: They were brothers, they were soul brothers. I feel right now that Kris is the closest link I have to my dad.

"I'd seen a lot of these photographs, but the ones that I hadn't seen before were really moving to me. They weren't just kind of stock Johnny Cash pictures, but showed some side of him, some depth, that hadn't really been captured before. And of course I really liked some ironic things, fun things, like him in those black-and-white loafers, and he's holding his Gibson, his Johnny Cash Gibson, and he's in the pale blue socks. It's just such an awesome picture— some kind of cross between rockabilly and jazz and the Kingston Trio."

As Rosanne has ventured there, this is mentioned to her: how her dad's music was relatively catholic through the years—hard to pigeon-hole as stone-cold "country." She says, "Absolutely. He was ecumenical, very much so. We liked that. He took my brother [half brother John Carter Cash, John and June's son] to Metallica. He took me to see Strawberry Alarm Clock when I was 15 years old. Talk about ecumenical! Totally ecumenical."

"Where did you go to see Strawberry Alarm Clock?" she is asked.

"It was in Hendersonville, at the Hendersonville High School. I remember liking them, and I remember visiting my dad for the summer and there was a really small crowd, and I and my dad sat in the front row."

"Did the band know who he was?"

IN THE LATER 1960s, Rosanne is at the far left, along with her sisters Kathy, Tara and Cindy. At the far right is her grandmother Carrie. This photo was taken in an age when folks just didn't say "Grandma, you had your eyes closed!" and then were able to take a second, corrective shot with the camera phone.

"Oh, hell yes."

"Did they have more than one song?"

She laughs and says, "Not really, no. Everybody knew 'Incense and Peppermints' and that was about it. But Dad enjoyed himself I think."

"He probably couldn't go anywhere in Hendersonville—or Tennessee—where they didn't know who he was, right? Was he the center of it when you went out as a family, or did he try to fade into the background?"

"No, no," Rosanne answers quickly, "He was the center, he was the center. He would decide on hot summer afternoons that we were going to the movies, and we would go from theater to theater. I was 11 or 12, or early teens or late teens even, and we would go to four movies in a day. Or he would decide that we were going roller-skating and he would rent the roller-skating rink."

"It's good being Johnny Cash!"

"Well, he was so famous he couldn't go anywhere and have his peace, so if he wanted to go anywhere with his kids and enjoy himself, he had to do those things."

"What about those summer photos at the lake house?" Rosanne is asked. "It looks like a magical time for a kid.

ROSANNE today has successful careers in singing and writing. Her most recent album, *The List,* features colaborations with many old friends, including Bruce Springsteen, on songs that her father once told her she simply needed to know.

In the movie [*Walk the Line*] they showed the lake house accurately, but here you people really are . . ."

"Well," she says. "A movie's a movie. The photos are real. But I remember it as almost *unreal.* It was idyllic for a kid in the summers. I can't tell you how great it was, everything about it. It was a perfect life, those summers— the pool and the boat and the southern cooks every afternoon at 4:30, and it was just the people who came in and out and my dad at the height of his health and power and orchestrating all of these great things for the kids to do, taking us to the farm or . . . The jeep riding was huge. Every day in the summer, there was a jeep ride."

It is suggested to Rosanne: "There's a photo of him with John Carter on his lap helping him drive [pages 114–115] and he looks so happy."

"Yeah, he was, he was—it was probably the happiest time of his life. And those are some of the best memories of my life."

"We have a lot of pictures of family reunions. What were those like?"

"The family gatherings?" She laughs again. "What were they like? Well, it depended if everyone was clean and sober. Some of them were great. In the late 1970s and early '80s, they were fantastic. But other times, some people would come in not the best shape, and that would blow things up.

"The pictures—I want to say one more thing about the pictures while we're talking about this. A couple of them from the drug years, it's so painful to see those: the gaunt ones. There are the ones in the studio [on pages 78 and 80–81, when he is recording the German-language version of "I Walk the Line" in 1965], and right near those, the one of him sitting in the lakeside room, it had to be the lakeside room, and that's maybe 1967. I would've been 12. And he had been gaunt in those studio photos, but now he had stopped using, and he was putting on weight and getting healthy again. So that is really interesting, in those two photos. It looks like: Here is a turning point. Those two years between those two photos, those were a couple of tough years. But you can see he's coming out of it, and by the next year, when all of us are outside, he looks 10 years younger."

She turns to another subject: "It's wonderful, too, looking at the pictures of my mother. There's the one of her getting on the plane and she's clearly pregnant [page 39]. I'm not sure who she's pregnant with, though. There's also this photo where my mom and dad are at a dinner table talking to someone. It's Mitch Miller [page 47], and my mother— the look she had on her face. I remember my parents talking about him. And the look on my mom's face, where she's just not buying what he has to say. Like he wants them to do something that she's not buying. She was like that."

That's the other side of these pictures, of course: the professional side of Johnny Cash the singer, not John Cash the father and husband. Rosanne indicates that in her family, which of course evolved into the even larger Carter-Cash clan, the two often overlapped. "At the lake house, or anywhere, there was always music, always music. When you couldn't say anything else, there was always music."

"Do you remember the legendary 'guitar pulls' in the lakeside room?"

"Yeah, I remember them—always in the lakeside room, as it was called. Some of those pictures in the big rooms at the lake house, they open a door into all that family history."

"Did you sing?'

"Yeah, I did, when I was starting to become a songwriter. And I still cringe to think of myself singing for some of those groups of people, with those songs I wrote. It was the hubris of youth. I don't know, I was 18 or 19, and the audience, well, I remember Billy Graham being there once, and I remember Tammy Wynette and George Jones and Roy Orbison and Mickey Newbury . . ."

"Those were kind people in your jury."

"Yes, yeah. Very kind people. It was hard for me to wrap my mind around it. I was really young, like 18, and learning how to play guitar and write songs. My dad was so encouraging. He would take me on stage with him and tell me that even the worst stuff I wrote was wonderful. He was the ultimate support. And as I got older and got a recording contract—which, by the way, he was instrumental in me getting, which I didn't learn until much later—I started pulling away a bit. I wanted to do it on my own, you know, and I wanted to work this out on my own, without people constantly referencing him in my work. He understood that, too. I think it may have hurt him a bit, but he understood it totally. And we got through that, the thing everyone goes through in their twenties, and then everything was just great. We would talk about music and politics every time we got together. We talked about music and politics all the time—and books . . . and books. Music and politics and books."

"It must have been nice," it is suggested, "to see him have that late-in-life renaissance as a singer."

"Renaissance?" Rosanne answers. "He had a lot of renaissances. That was one of the key character traits of my dad: He was like a phoenix. He would go down really dark and deep and come back. He did that so many times in his life. And after the last few years when he was so sick, the music really kept him alive, and it was his final burst—his final burst of genius. And some geniuses do that, you know, they don't let it crush them, the addiction or the illness or the whatever, and . . ."

"I saw him a lot, a lot, in those last years," she continues. "It was good. The family today? Well, Tara, my younger sister, she's out in Portland with two teenage boys and we're as close as any sisters can be. Our boys love each other like brothers. My other two sisters and half brother: We're close like any adults are. Rosie, June's daughter, is dead, as you know. It's hard, the passage of time. I'm still close to Etta Grant, Marshall's wife.

"The house [by the lake] is gone, as you know. The cabin's still there. John Carter still lives in Hendersonville, and he keeps up the recording cabin, and he records there. But that's it: the cabin, and their graves. They're buried there, and it's heartbreaking.

"The lake house, I think about it now, and it's like a dream and a myth. I wrote about the fires once. It's so weird. Roy Orbison's house was the next house down the road, and it burned down. And ours. And . . ."

"Well, there certainly are a lot of memories."

OHN
ORE "JOHNNY"

YES, HE WAS JOHN before Johnny, and in fact he was "J.R." before John, as we will shortly learn. Here is the future legend at 11 years old in 1942. At this point the family had already moved from Kingsland, Arkansas, to Dyess, and J.R. is already a six-year veteran of singing alongside his parents and siblings (he had six brothers and sisters in all) while working in the cotton fields.

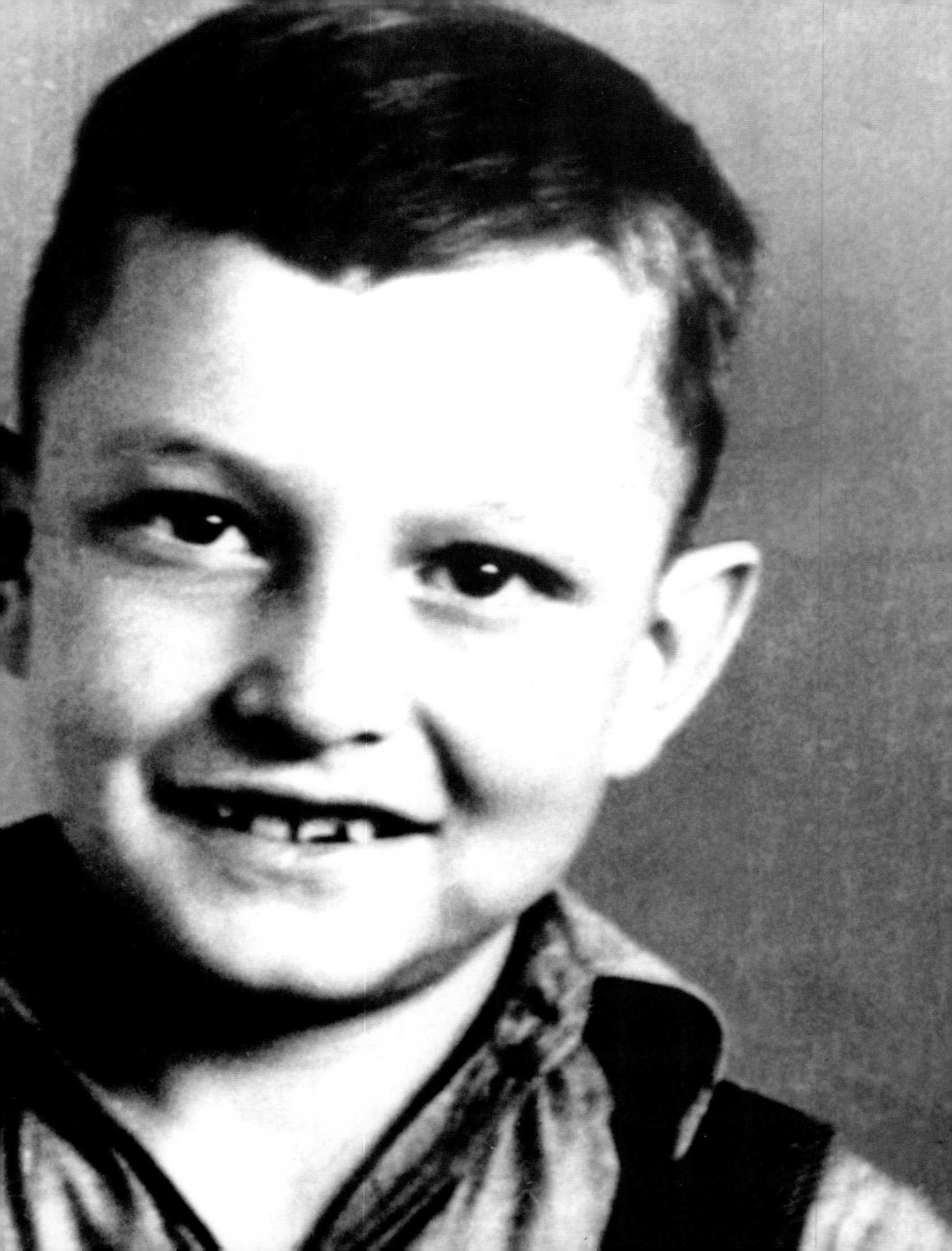

ON THE PORCH of the house in Dyess circa 1943, this is *most* of the Cash clan. But where's J.R.? Well, taking the photo. In Arkansas, everyone knew him as J.R. That's how he knew himself—in fact, it was his real name. His parents, Ray (in the hat) and Carrie (far left), couldn't think of a suitable name for the fourth of their eventual seven children, and so they called him J.R. Working in the cotton fields of Dyess from the age of five, the boy answered only to calls of J.R. Meanwhile, he soaked up the Depression-era travails of his family and friends. Clearly, he filed these away, for later, they would emerge in his songs. The family farm was flooded more than once, and "Johnny" Cash would sing of this in "Five Feet High and Rising."

J.R. was greatly affected by the death of his older brother Jack in a 1944 table-saw accident. Both boys and Carrie had a foreboding that morning, and she urged Jack to skip work cutting wood and go fishing with J.R. But Jack knew the family needed the money, and he reported for duty. Johnny Cash wrote much later that he looked forward to meeting his brother in the afterlife, and he commemorated Jack throughout his life. When he enlisted in the U.S. Air Force in 1950, he was told that initials alone would not do—he needed a proper name. He chose "John R. Cash," and if he felt this brought him yet closer to his late brother, that's exactly the kind of spiritual connection that would always be important to this man, a seeker all his days. In any event, this would now be Johnny Cash's "real name"; the world would know him by his stage name, Johnny, but he would always be called John by his friends and later family members (the Arkansas folks still called him J.R.). As for that family, from oldest to youngest the kids were Roy, Louise, Jack, J.R., Reba, Joanne and Tommy. This youngest would also be a successful country music artist and, now in his 70s, continues to sing—carrying on, with Rosanne, John Carter Cash and others, the family legacy.

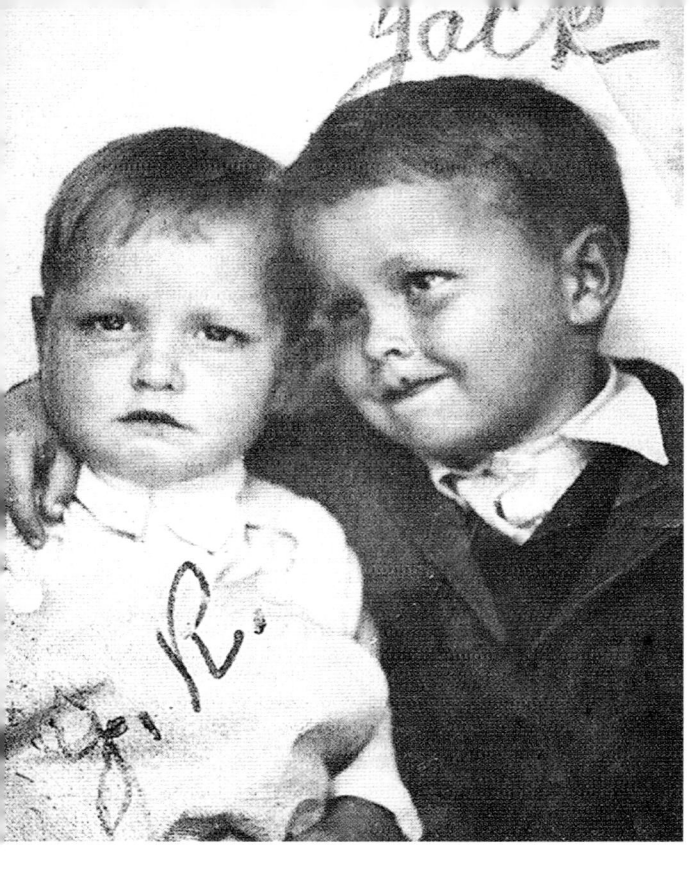

J.R. AND JACK, seen at left when J.R. is still a toddler circa 1936, are close as brothers and as boyhood friends, and would be linked eternally by tragedy. Below: The Cash family in Dyess in 1949, from left: Roy, Carrie, Louise, Tommy, Ray, Reba, Joanne and J.R. Opposite: Joanne, J.R. and Tommy. Both of these Cash boys did stints in the service: J.R., changing his name to John, in the Air Force, and Tommy in the Army, after which, already a veteran of a high school band, he played some with Hank Williams Jr. Tommy's biggest hit, in 1969, would be "Six White Horses," a song dedicated to the two assassinated Kennedy brothers and to Martin Luther King Jr.

CASH FAMILY COLLECTION, ARKANSAS STATE UNIVERSITY (3)

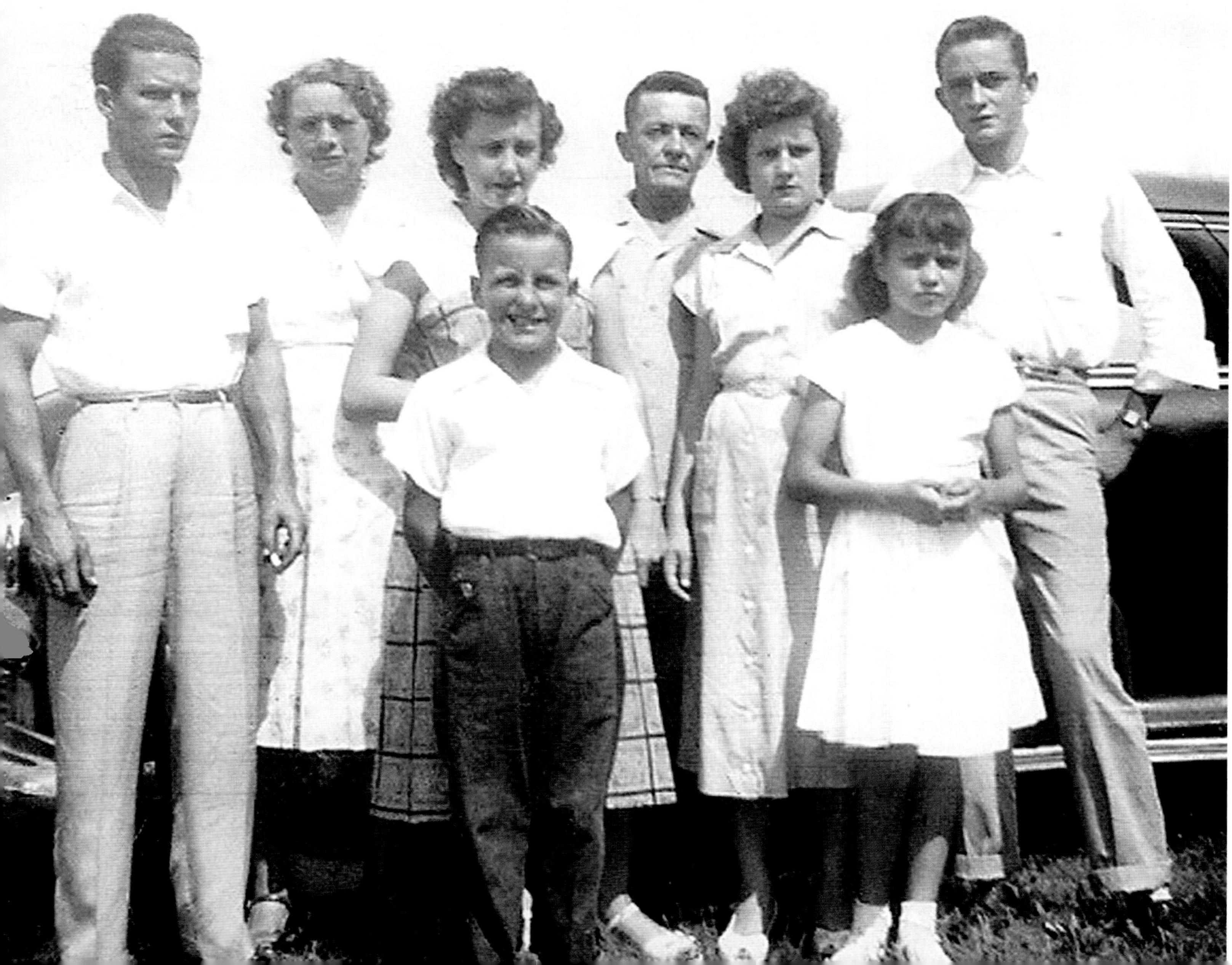

J. R. Cash
Vice-Pres

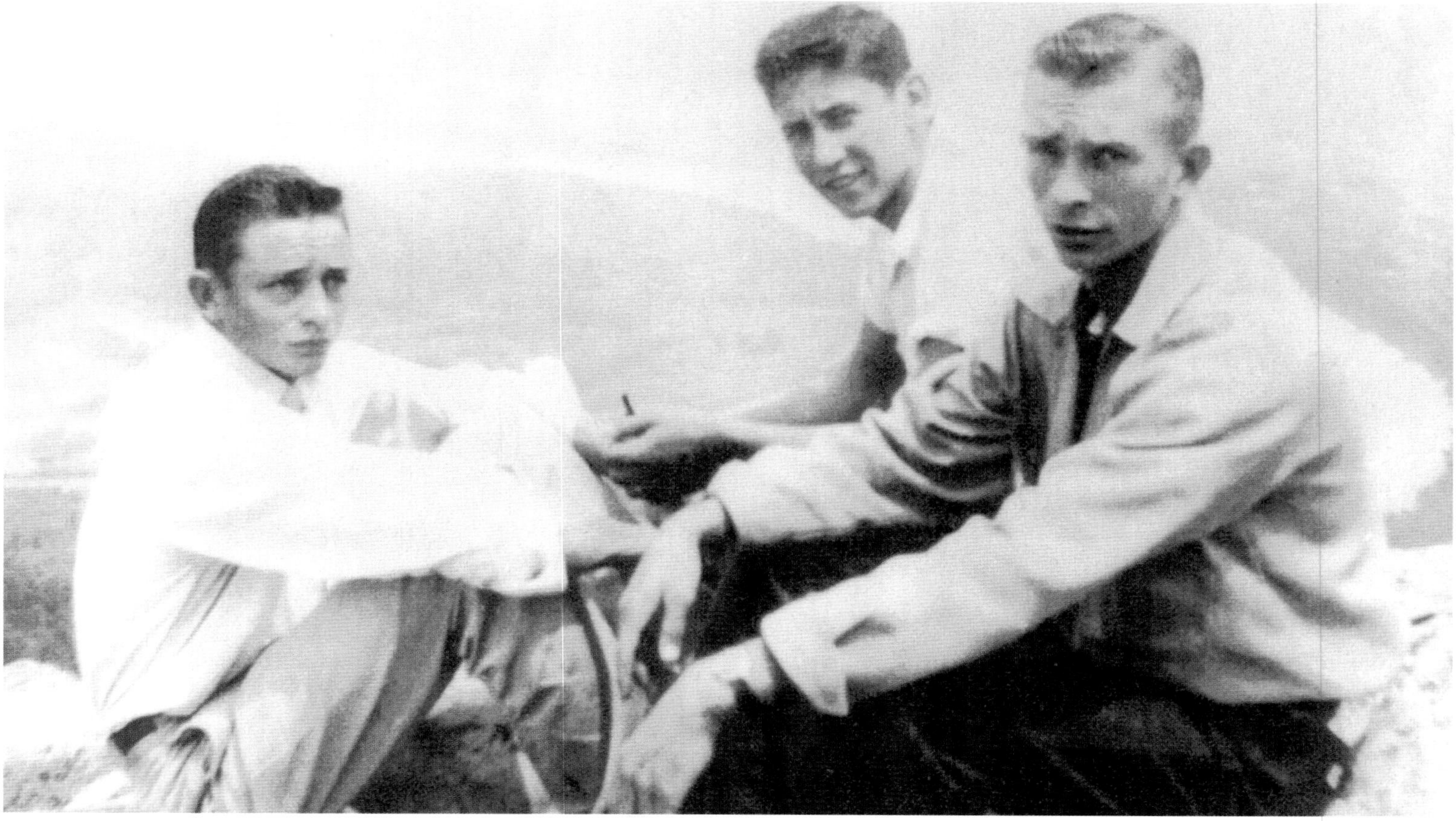

GAB ARCHIVE/REDFERNS/GETTY

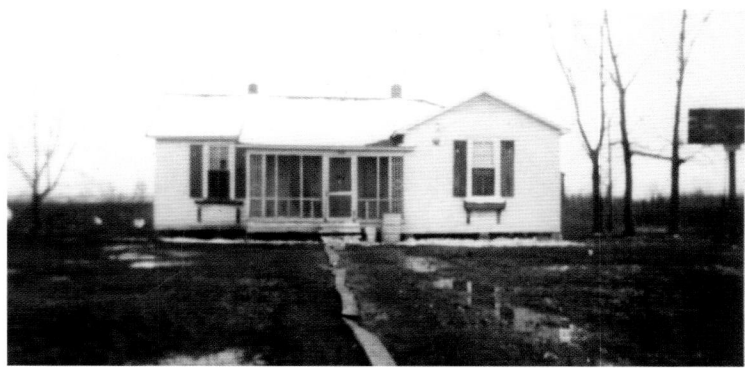

MORE PICTURES FROM DYESS. On the opposite page: J.R. Cash, high school vice president, class of 1950. Top: J.R. Cash, W.R. Criswell and Dorsey Fincher on a senior trip. Above: The Cash family home circa 1952. By this point "John" had met Vivian Liberto at a roller-skating rink in July of 1951. They were immediately starry-eyed: he a 19-year-old service member in training (he was shortly to be deployed to Germany), she a lovely 17-year-old Texan. They dated for three weeks until John flew to Europe, then, over three years, wrote literally hundreds of love letters. They wed, almost as soon as John was discharged from the Air Force, on August 7, 1954, at St. Ann Catholic Church in San Antonio. At right, John performs with Luther Perkins, who represents as well as anyone the transition from Arkansas to Tennessee. John and Vivian moved to Memphis in 1954. There he sold appliances and took courses to be a radio announcer. As a sideline, he played guitar with Perkins and Marshall Grant, the Tennessee Two (the act would later be called the Tennessee Three, after they added a drummer). The rest—which would be country music history—remained to be written.

CASH FAMILY COLLECTION, ARKANSAS STATE UNIVERSITY (3)

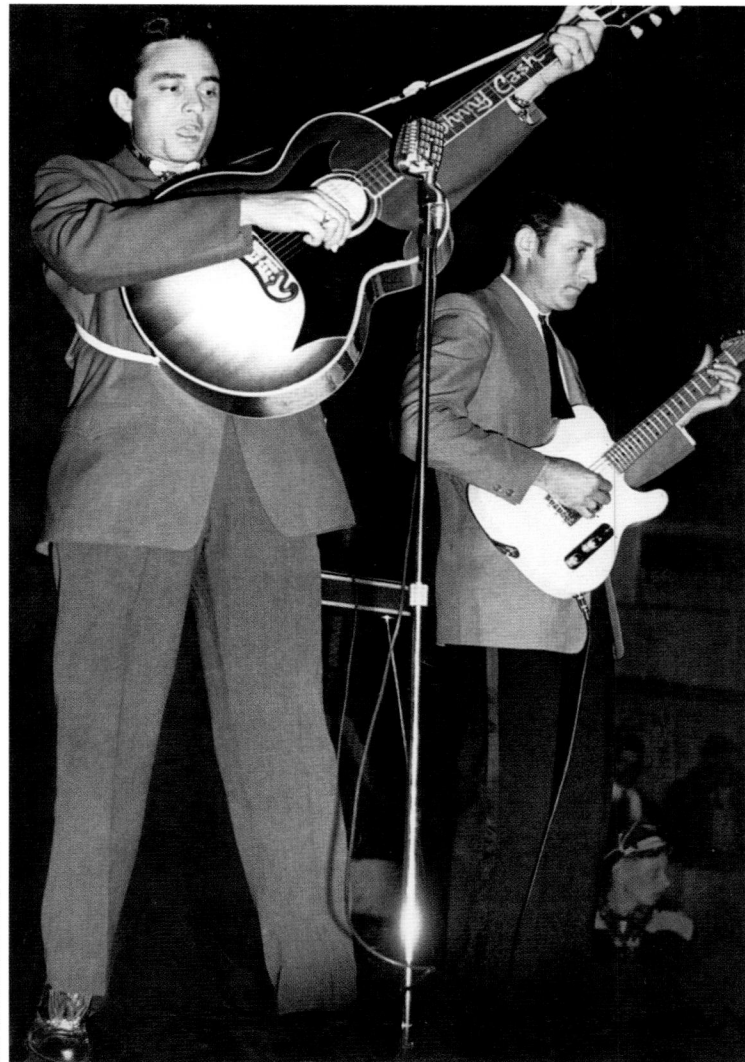

FROM MEMPHIS TO NASHVILLE

AND NOW WE ENTER the great stash of photography from the Sony Archives, some of which is bizarre and some of which John might have wished destroyed before his death. Would this be Exhibit A? Probably not; there's even more embarrassing (if fun) stuff ahead. The outtakes of publicity shoots, when the record companies were trying to figure out precisely how to position an artist—playing with whether this guy or that gal might be "crossover"—are always irresistible. Johnny was certainly going to be a rockabilly or country performer, but here he looks like he was auditioning for Tito Puente's band.

CRPS

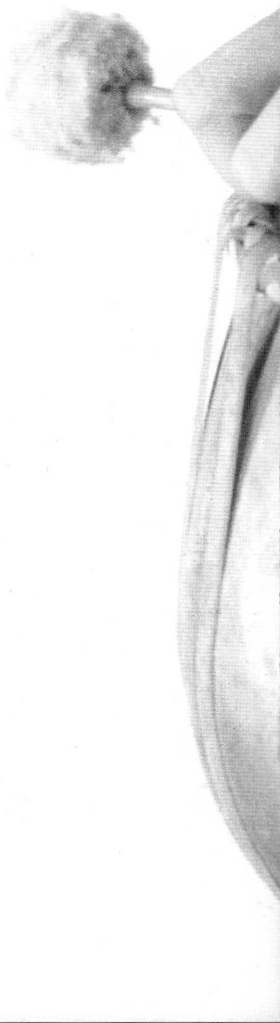

THIS FAMOUS PHOTOGRAPH is the opposite of a rarity in that it has been seen a thousand times, but then again it is something of a rarity because you have these four very famous guys, and there aren't even four pictures of them together to commemorate what happened that December day in Memphis. As mentioned in our introduction, the photograph needs to be presented in a book such as ours: as a signpost, as a crucial episode in the story that was now becoming the Johnny Cash saga.

How had he come to this point in time, where he was included that afternoon in what would later be called the Million Dollar Quartet? The same way he had become "Johnny"—through the auspices of legendary producer Sam Phillips.

One day in Memphis, John had taken a deep breath and gone down to the Sun Records studio from which he and (from left in the photo) Jerry Lee Lewis, Carl Perkins and Elvis Presley would emerge as stars. "I went and knocked on that door and was turned away," he later remembered in a story he told in slightly different ways at different times. "I called back for an interview three or four times, was turned away. So one morning I found out what time the man [Phillips] went to work. I went down with my guitar and sat on his steps until he got there. And when he got there I introduced myself . . . Evidently, he woke up on the right side of the bed that morning. He said, 'Come on in. Let's listen.'" Phillips wasn't taken with Cash's gospel stuff, but said, "Come back tomorrow and bring some musicians." When John returned with his Tennessee Two mates Perkins and Grant and some rockabilly material, including "Hey Porter" and later "Cry, Cry, Cry," Phillips came fully around. When he was pressing these first records in 1955, the producer said to himself and to his latest protégé that the name "Johnny" was catchier than "John." And that was that.

The next year—on December 4, 1956, to cite the historical date—Elvis dropped by Sun during a Carl Perkins recording session; Jerry Lee Lewis was playing piano. Cash was also there, and when the four of them started fooling around with gospel tunes, Phillips left the tapes running. Those sessions are today immortal, with "Down by the Riverside" perhaps the highlight. Unfortunately, our man John didn't sing on that number.

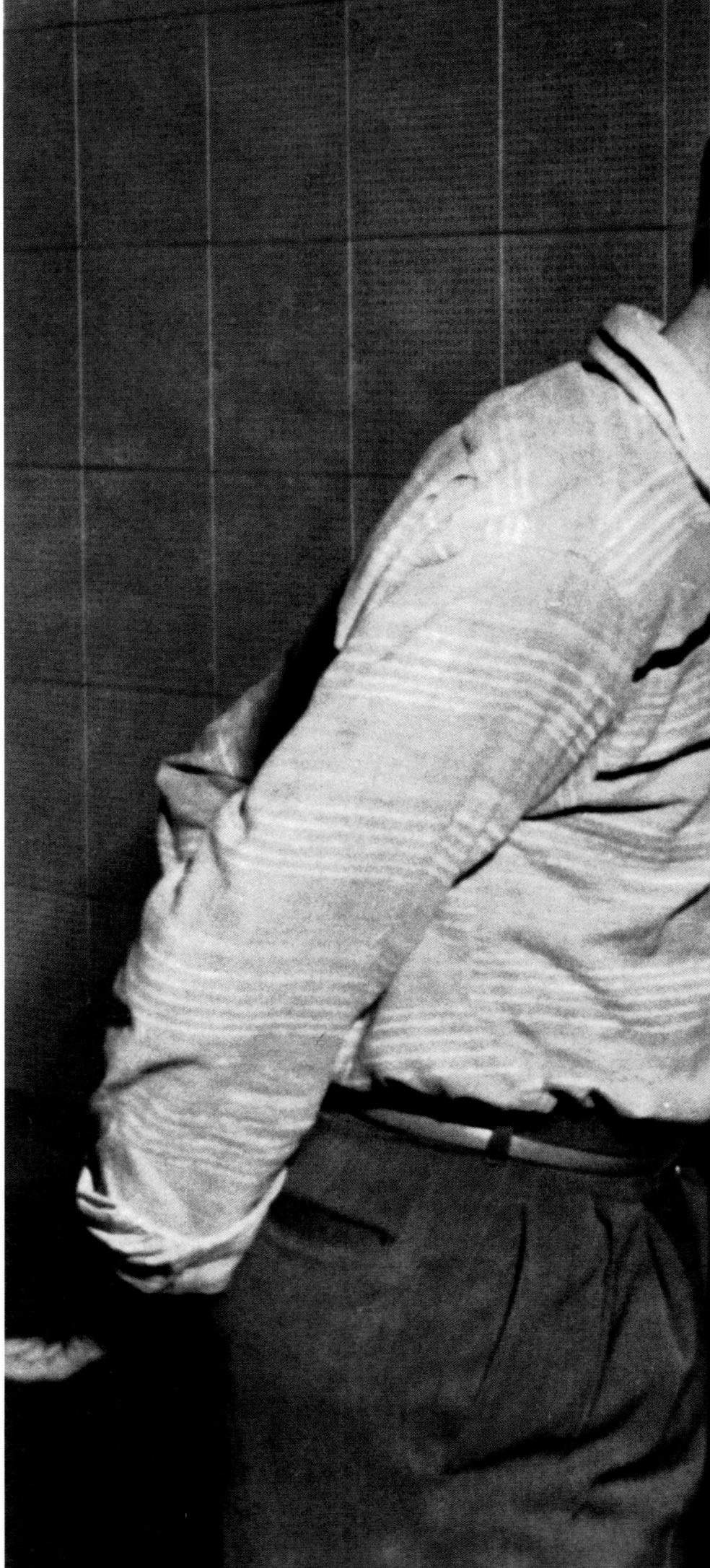

ARCHIVE PHOTOS

BEFORE ELVIS LEFT SUN, the going was good—and thrilling—for all concerned, as Phillips sought to pull nothing but gems out of his charges. John once recalled to writer Robert Hilburn, whose biography of Cash comes out later this year: "Sam didn't have a clock in the studio. He didn't make me feel like I was spending anybody's money by just singing new songs. After an hour or two, he'd say, 'Okay, what else you got? Let's keep going till we get your best.' I loved that in a producer. That's what Sam did with all of us at Sun. He tried to find the uniqueness in each of us."

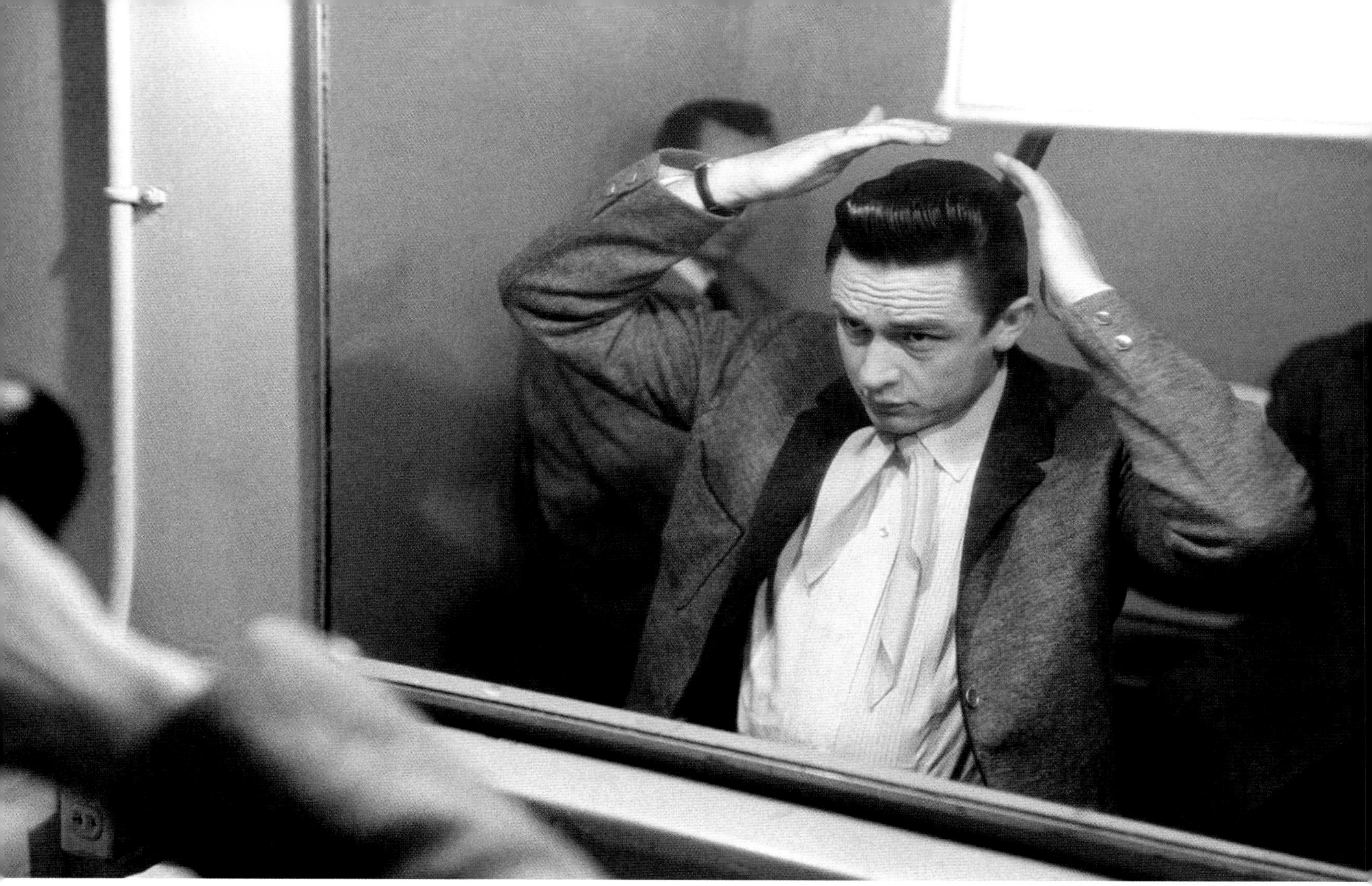

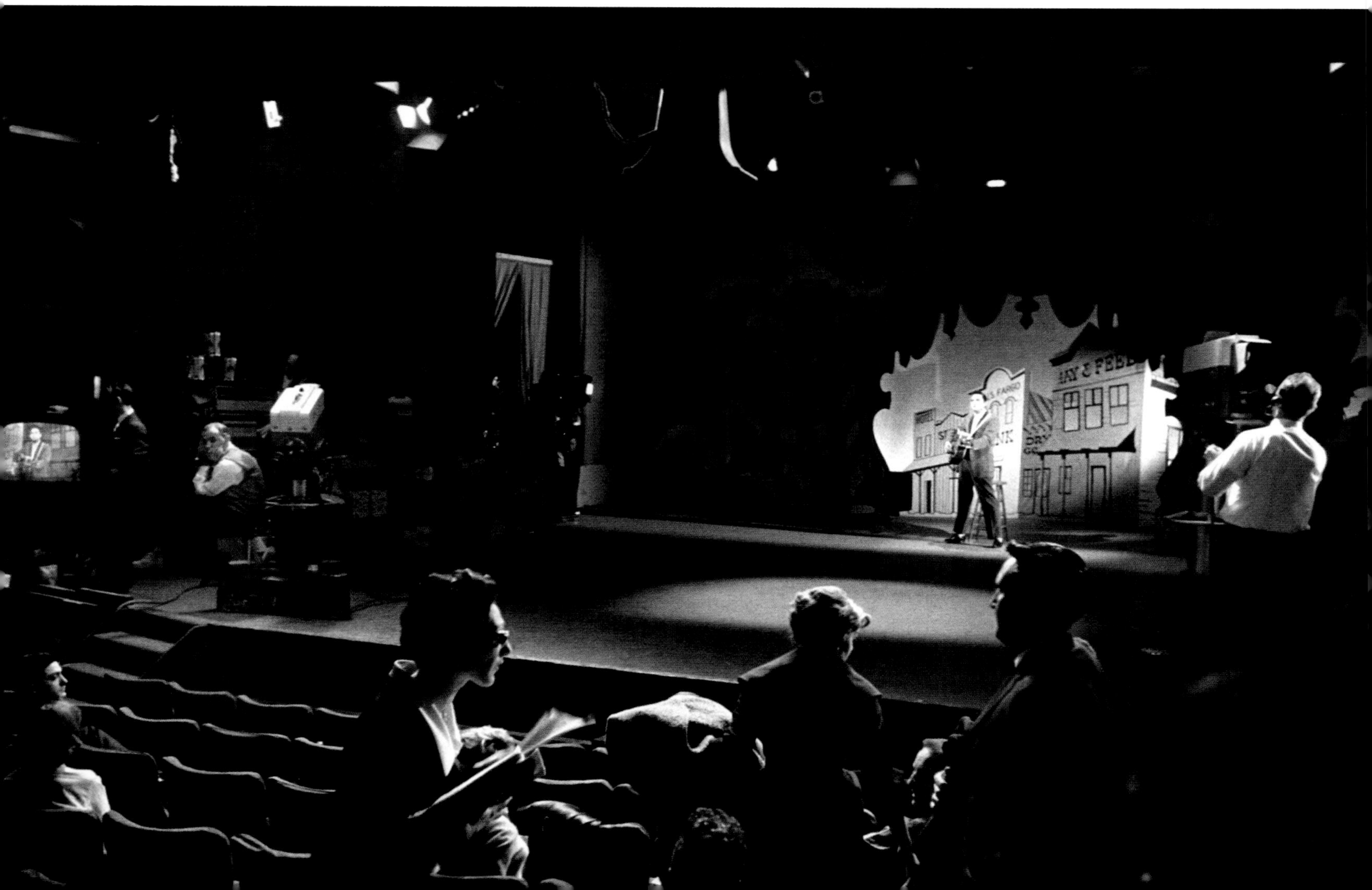

THE GIGS GOT BETTER. Cash's third release on Sun, the 1956 single "I Walk the Line" (which was meant for Vivian) backed with "Get Rhythm," established him as a rising star. His first performance with the Tennessee Two, seemingly only moments before, had been in a church basement playing for elderly ladies. Now he was being booked into the biggest halls in Memphis and was taking his act on the road—the *Louisiana Hayride,* the Grand Ole Opry, even (on these pages) *The Dick Clark Show.*

GUY GILLETTE

THE FANS were pressing in, and with their omnipresence came the temptations that many a music star before Johnny Cash—and after him— has known. He was hardly a saint; he never claimed to be one. He may have sung that he was walking the line, but he never swore it on a Bible. His first marriage would endure more than a decade into his stardom, but it wouldn't be easy. Early on there were the affairs, and a close friendship with one woman in particular. In 1955, backstage at a concert at the Grand Ole Opry in Nashville, John was introduced to a young woman named June, a daughter in the first family of country music, the Carters. John and June got on fine. They quickly became pals, and would never be out each other's sight.

DON HUNSTEIN

IT'S NOT ALWAYS EASY or altogether honest to put together a showbiz career. As we see on the next four pages, when the cameras are sent in by the handlers to chronicle the life of a star, that star must smile, pose, suggest a certain faux intimacy, even show a bit of beefcake in the hotel room. If there are other women besides the wife, if there are very late nights fueled by booze and drugs, if those late nights are becoming a problem—all of this must go unsaid, and certainly unseen. (Just by the way, though: John Carter Cash tells LIFE today that booze was never the problem; drugs were. "Dad had very little problem with alcohol," he says. "His thing was the pills.")

Of these photos, the color portrait here from 1958 is, as Rosanne Cash has said, a standout (how about those two-tone shoes!). The following pictures depict an exciting time in the life of John and Vivian Cash: cross-country trips to California, hotel rooms on someone else's dime. In the tumultuous dozen years of their marriage, there certainly was joy—they had four daughters: Rosanne, Kathy, Cindy and Tara—and John became a star. But meantime he developed those drug addictions and generally carried on. These were states of affairs that couldn't be hidden from Vivian.

JOHN HAMILTON

THE COUNTRY OF country music was also, in the late 1950s and early '60s (and still proudly today) the country of such things as stock car racing and big-time college football, and before too very long Johnny Cash could fill a stadium as readily as Fireball Roberts or 'Bama versus Auburn. Here he's alongside Luther Perkins in 1958, and this is precisely the kind of "who cares?" photo that got buried more than a half century ago but that speaks volumes—and is a lot of fun to look at—today. In 1958, Johnny, knowing he was hot (as that year ended, he was the third-highest-selling country artist in America, and was appearing nationwide, prime time, on such programs as *The Jackie Gleason Show*), followed Elvis's lead and left the comforting confines of Sun Records and its nurturing paterfamilias Sam Phillips to sign a big-money deal with Columbia Records, where he would remain for much of his career (just as Elvis would stick with RCA). Many boardroom negotiations later, Columbia is today part of Sony—and that's why this precious legacy of photography is available to us all in this book.

KXLA
POPULARITY AWARD

Johnny Cash

The most popular recording artist
of 1958 as selected by the
listeners of KXLA
the Western music station,
Pasadena

IN A MORE INNOCENT AGE a popularity award from one of many country music radio stations was something to show off. (Today, if it's not a CMA trophy or a Grammy, forget it.) Above: En route from one gig to another are John and Vivian, certainly happy to be booked on a major airline. In that era, when rock 'n' roll or country artists had become big enough to be in demand nationwide, they quite often had to start puddle-jumping by plane—any plane. Buddy Holly, Ritchie Valens and Jiles Perry "J.P." Richardson Jr. (better known as the Big Bopper) were killed on the "day the music died" in 1959, and country's queen, Patsy Cline, died in Tennessee in 1963, when the Piper she was traveling in went down. In the first of those two famous crashes, Waylon Jennings, who was playing bass in Buddy Holly's Crickets, gave up his seat on the plane to the Big Bopper—and was thus spared. He and Johnny Cash were already friends, and would become better ones, eventually collaborating in the Highwaymen. We'll meet Waylon plenty in these pages.

THE MAN IN BLACK was sartorially inclined that way early on, as you can tell here and also by several of the photos on the last few pages. (Then again, in the next couple of pictures he looks like he could have become known as the Man in Plaid. We can all agree that he made the correct choice, yes?) In 1958, now with Columbia Records, Johnny had a very strange No. 1 country single—and it wasn't even a Columbia release. Sun Records, which would continue to issue older Johnny Cash recordings into the '60s, thought there was potential in "Ballad of a Teenage Queen," and they thought correctly. Johnny's subsequent No. 1s for Columbia were much closer to the bone, and hewed to the direction he wanted to take—"Don't Take Your Guns to Town," for instance—but the larger point was, Johnny Cash, whatever he sang, was hot and getting hotter. In the next decade, during which time Cash became the biggest country crossover star to that point (and maybe the biggest ever—Garth Brooks and Taylor Swift and Johnny's friend Willie Nelson included—when you factor in John's popular variety show, of which we will learn more shortly), Columbia sold more than 20 million Johnny Cash albums worldwide. In the early '60s, there was nothing that could stop him, unless he stopped himself.

DON HUNSTEIN

JOHN, SMILING, gives some fans a thrill—and a picture. He's happy, he's successful, but he's in trouble. The long tours and late nights got to him early, and in 1957 during a road trip to Jacksonville, Florida, he began to take amphetamines to stay awake. That addiction and a second to barbiturates would last a decade, and there would be others, some even worse; he "tried every drug there was to try," in this period. Onstage at the Grand Ole Opry, he once strafed the footlights with the microphone stand, shattering glass and causing wonderment and fright. He was busted in El Paso for buying pills in Mexico, busted again in LaFayette, Georgia. Meantime, of course, he generated more hits, and became an even bigger star. "Ring of Fire" and "Understand Your Man"—both of which were surely autobiographical, and reflecting his introspection while only slightly concealing his self-disgust— both went to No. 1 on the country charts; "Ring of Fire" replicated the transcendent performance of "I Walk the Line," entering the pop Top 20 as well. But was John still rising? Or was he heading for a fall? Only he knew. Rather: Only he could supply an answer.

AS BIG AS HE WAS becoming, he never forgot where he was from, and he was unfailingly generous to other artists—something that would become a Johnny Cash hallmark. In a 1994 interview, he told LIFE a charming story: "I recorded 'Orange Blossom Special' in the mid-'60s, and in those days everybody that recorded it claimed the 'arrangement' because no one knew who wrote it. But Mother Maybelle Carter was at the session, and I asked her, 'Do you know who really wrote "Orange Blossom Special"?' She said, 'Sure I do. Ervin Rouse and his brother Gordon.' And I said, 'Where are they?' She said, 'Last time I heard, they were in Florida.' It was the only clue I had. I called a disc jockey down there named Cracker Jim Brooker, and I asked Cracker Jim, 'Did you ever hear of Ervin Rouse?' And he said, 'Aw, I know Ervin. He lives with the Seminoles out in the swamp, and he makes swamp buggies for a living. I said, 'You got any idea how I could talk to him?' And he said, 'Sure. I'll announce it on the air: "Ervin, call me and I'll give you Johnny Cash's number."' It wasn't an hour till Ervin Rouse called me from some little settlement in the swamps. I said, 'Ervin, I happen to be coming to Miami on tour. Would you come to my show and do "Orange Blossom Special" with me?' He and Gordon came in the clothes they worked in. I brought Ervin up to play the fiddle, and he absolutely killed them. At the end of the song, they were applauding and he literally got down on his knees. He was such a sweet, humble man."

DON HUNSTEIN

THERE'S NO MISTAKING Johnny Cash, whether it's the husky-dusky voice, the bluesy beats, the boom-chicka-boom rhythm on the up-tempo numbers or, visually, the dangerous mien, the hue of the clothing (yikes! here we have . . . *white*!) or the guitar riding up to his chin. Here and on the next six pages: The man at work once he had become a star. Above is a business session with Mitch Miller, then an A&R man for Columbia, with Vivian sitting in. On the pages following these, we will discuss Johnny in the studio for Columbia during the hit-making days—and elsewhere, afterward—in a bit more depth.

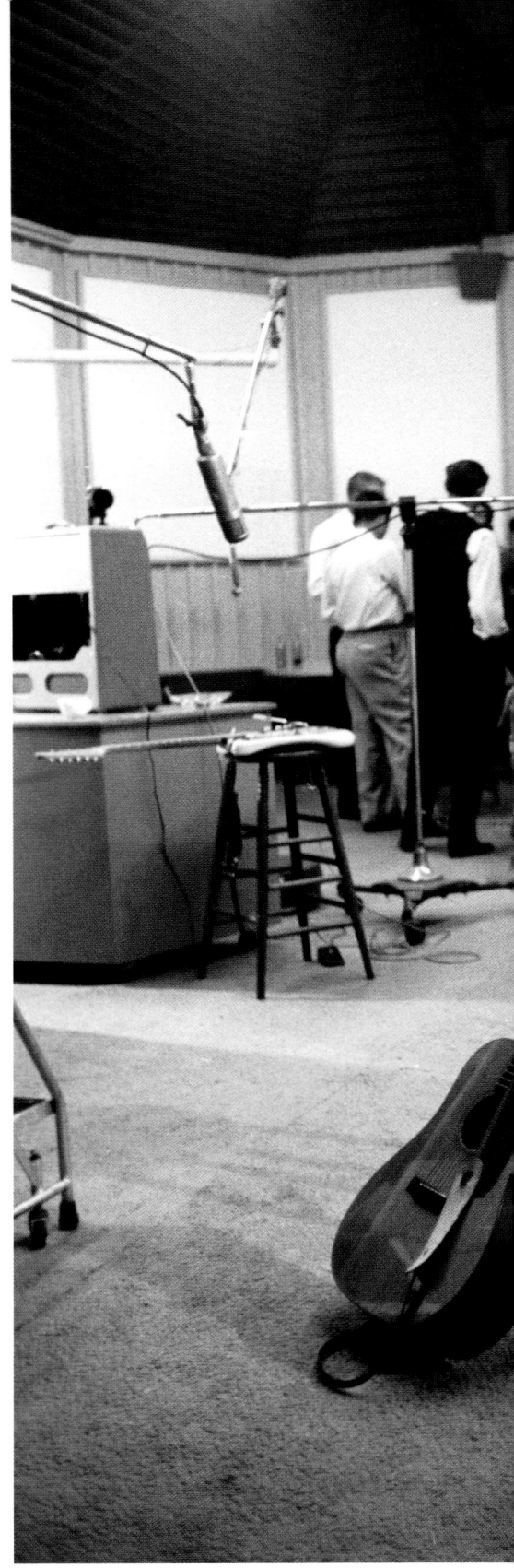

IN THE STUDIO, whatever studio that might be in whichever period of his long career, Johnny was a consummate pro and at ease. His friend Willie Nelson legendarily recorded his masterpiece *Red Headed Stranger* in a day and a half, and has said that most of his recordings were made on a first or second take—third at the most. Johnny wasn't quite that carefree, but he too came prepared, and always checked his ego at the door. "I don't know if he was aware of the magnitude of his presence, but pretty much anybody who came into contact with him was intimidated by him, for the most part," said Rick Rubin, who years later produced Johnny's acclaimed last sessions, the so-called American Recordings. "But he was just such a humble person, in a few lines of casual conversation he was able to make everyone feel okay. Again, I don't know how much of that was preplanned, or done on purpose, but I saw it happen a lot. It may have just been a natural urge to put people at ease; it may not have had anything to do with celebrity. But it definitely worked, in terms of just taking the intimidation factor down, and making people feel comfortable." Even in the days when heavy drug abuse was the ruin of many a public performance, Johnny could

still pull it together in the studio, as we see here and on the next four pages in pictures made in 1959. He always focused intently on the lyric, said Rubin—he knew exactly what he was trying to convey when he sang each song, even if the message was based on the suggestion of someone else. It has often been said that you can hear this on the American Recordings, but really: You can hear it on all of them. There's a remarkable double-disc called *Personal File,* a collection of 49 songs his family stumbled upon after Cash's death: recordings he had made by himself, alone with his guitar, in his home studio. "There were a lot of songs that I wrote when I first started out in my musical career that I never recorded for one reason or another, either I didn't feel good about them . . . or maybe the record company didn't feel like they were up to par or something," Cash said into the microphone about these remarkable songs that no one knew he was about to record. "But some of those songs must have had something, because I still remember them. And every once in a while, when I'm driving along in the car, I sing them over and over to myself." He finally sang them for posterity, and we are all the luckier for it.

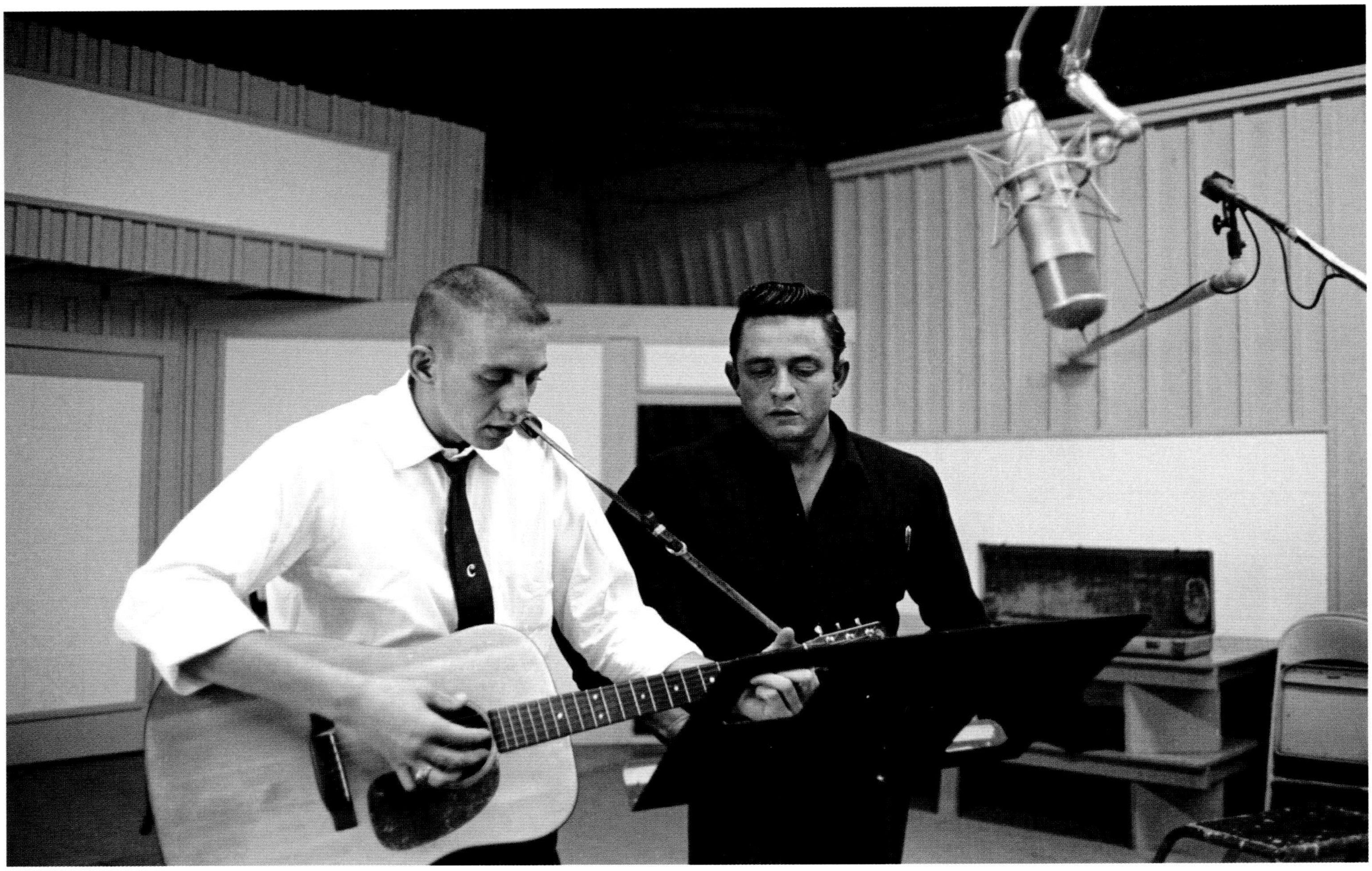

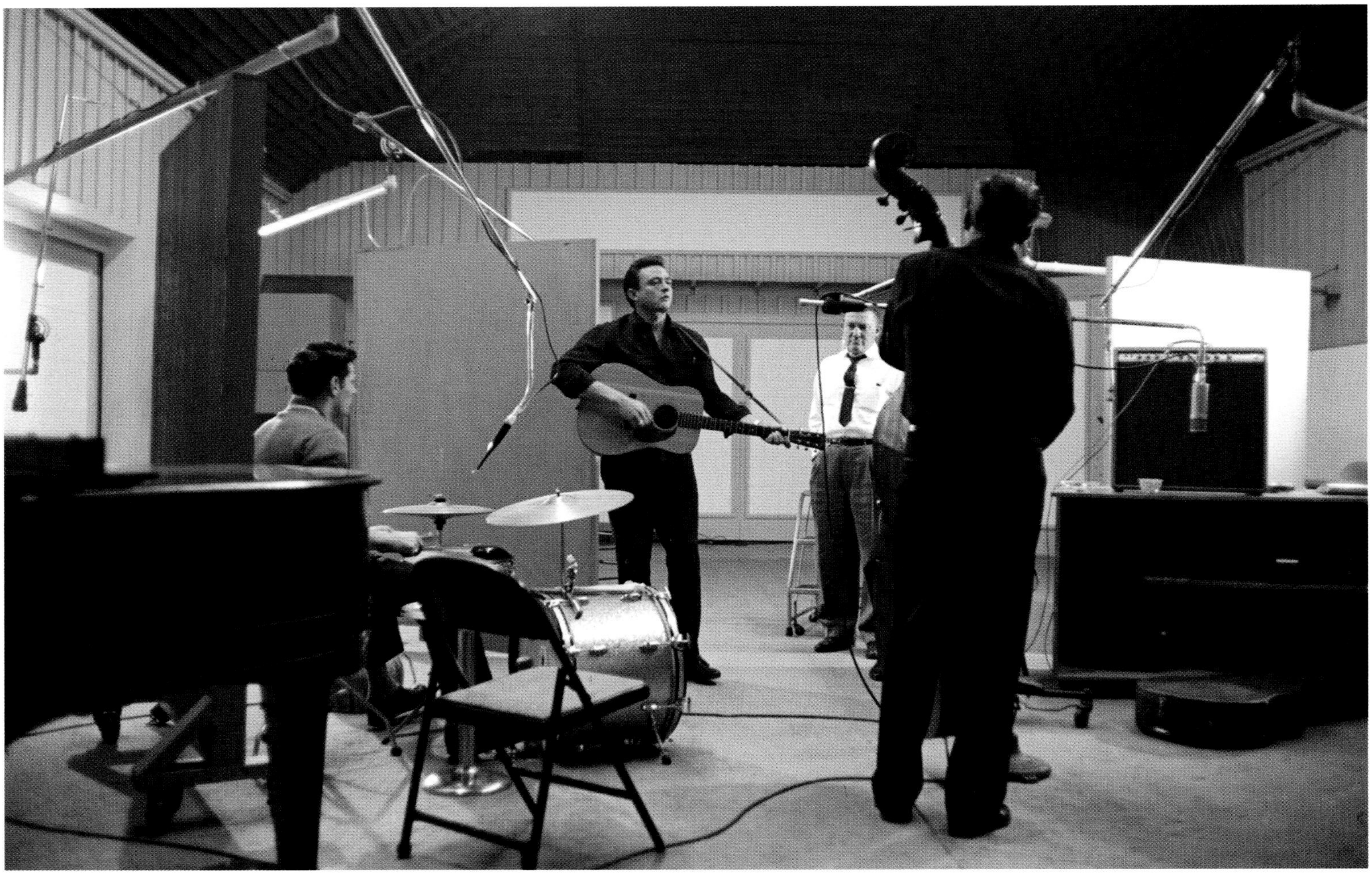

DON HUNSTEIN (3)

APPEARANCES can deceive, and they do to a degree in the family portrait on this page inside the Cashes' new home in Los Angeles, and the color one made outdoors that is shown on the following two pages. This looks like a happy family—the very happiest. Vivian and John are trying hard to insulate the children from their troubles; they are sometimes succeeding. "We were rich in love, but dirt poor," Vivian later wrote, looking back to the earliest days of their relationship. "We woke up every day never knowing where our next dollar would come from. We just struggled together, blissfully unconcerned about the future." Johnny was the one who had brought the problems on, of course, and we've already alluded to that in these pages. Suffice to say: After the $50,000 bonus from Columbia Records in 1958 and then the overtures from the movie studios, they moved to Southern California with their three daughters (Rosanne, Kathy and Cindy; and soon after, a fourth, Tara, was born, in 1961). The house seen here was in Encino—bought from Johnny Carson, no less—and later there would be a ranch. Vivian sensed a "dangerous current" after the move to California, but this can translate prosaically into drugs and life on the road. The good news: The children grew up healthy, and as happy as could be.

DON HUNSTEIN

DON HUNSTEIN (2)

THE PAST, PRESENT AND FUTURE were all in play when the Cash family left Tennessee for California. He's a big star but not the very biggest; he has settled out West but is still traveling to Nashville to play the Grand Ole Opry. He has a passel of hits in his satchel, any of which he can trot out on a given night. He has dipped his toe into acting on TV (playing "Pratt" in a series called *The Rebel* and "Bo Braddock" in *The Deputy*) and even in the movies ("Johnny Cabot" in *Five Minutes to Live*). What the future holds is anyone's guess. We now know for a certainty: No one could possibly have guessed it.

JOHN WAS by this point known to the whole world as Johnny—introducing himself nightly with "Hello. I'm Johnny Cash," a simple line that, in the 1960s and '70s, became the country equivalent of "Ladies and gentlemen, the Rolling Stones." He was on top of the world, even as he was bottoming out. In this next period, he would find salvation of a sort, thanks to June and God, while learning only too well that demons are tough to shake and hard to keep at bay.

A KING OF
COUNTRY

THERE WAS A WONDERFUL moment honoring another Columbia Records artist—actually, two of them, Simon & Garfunkel—that speaks to the photograph at left, and to much of the ecumenism that John would stress and vigorously defend as his career in country music progressed. When Paul Simon and Art Garfunkel were inducted as a duo into the Rock and Roll Hall of Fame in 1990, Simon said during his acceptance remarks, "We fell in love with rock 'n' roll when we were 12 years old, 13 years old, when there was one station in New York, WINS. And used to hear this music—I mean, one song would be Ray Charles, 'Hallelujah, I Love Her So,' and then it would be Johnny Cash, 'I Walk the Line,' and then it would be Frankie Lymon and 'Why Do Fools Fall in Love?' and then Carl Perkins, and then maybe Ruth Brown, and the Moonglows, and the Penguins, Joe Turner blues—I mean, a diversity—a rich diversity of music that would be impossible to hear on any format radio today." Later in his speech, after detailing his and Garfunkel's early struggles as an act called "Tom & Jerry" and then their split, Simon continued: "We got back together again in 1964 when Goddard Lieberson signed us to Columbia Records, and we owe Goddard our thanks for that, and also for the fact that he interceded on our behalf, and stopped the A&R department from naming our group Catchers in the Rye. And he allowed us to use our real names, something which would have been an impossibility in the '50s, for somebody to use names that were so ethnically identifiable as Simon and Garfunkel. We owe Goddard a great deal of thanks for that."

Goddard Lieberson is the man seated at right in this photograph, president of Columbia from 1956 to 1971 and then again from 1973 to 1975. He obviously was instrumental in signing and keeping Johnny Cash as well as Simon & Garfunkel (he is seen here, in 1965, with Don Law, head of Columbia's country music division). Lieberson allowed Cash all the freedom that he granted Simon & Garfunkel and all the many others, and his interesting story will be told further on the pages immediately following.

AGAIN, Law is at left, Lieberson at right. Lieberson was perhaps the most important record exec in the world—he had been instrumental in the switch from 78 RPM records to 33 ⅓ albums, and, having studied as a composer, this suave aristocrat held all-encompassing sway in the classical music universe. At Columbia in the '60s and '70s, he was required to handle it all, from Dylan to Santana to Blood, Sweat & Tears to his Carnegie Hall stalwarts (and pals) to Tony Bennett to Barbra Streisand to Miles Davis to folks like Johnny Cash, hanging out in Nashville. Lieberson professed to be greatly interested in Cash's career—certainly he professed such whenever posing with a gold record (here, in 1965)— and he might well have been, for he did renegotiate John's contract when the artist found himself, for no admissible reason, in need of quick money. Cash, for his part, referred to the debonair Lieberson—who was married to a ballet dancer and left his most lasting mark by producing original cast recordings of great musicals, including Rodgers and Hart's *Pal Joey* and *The Boys from Syracuse*—as the "Great White Father." To emphasize the original point: It is telling that John could get along with people like Lieberson as well as Waylon and Willie and Paul Simon and Bob Dylan and Joni Mitchell and . . . Well, it just didn't matter. Except that it mattered greatly, as we will see.

DON HUNSTEIN

DON HUNSTEIN

IT'S FUNNY: Back in the day, stars used to allow photographers into their homes; they are far more wary, far more encased, and do much less of this today. And yet magazine and record-album editors and designers seemed to prefer the elaborately staged portraits or, if they did choose shots from the "home shoot," obvious set-ups with Dad or Mom goofing with the kids. So many of the real gems went unseen, or perhaps wound up in the artist's family albums. This photograph is from 1960, at his home in California. Throughout life, John spent many of his best hours just like this (as the *Personal File* discs prove): communing with his guitar, his songs, his thoughts, his worries—and whomever else he might summon.

SUBJECTS THAT HAVE an edge today weren't necessarily so politically charged in 1960 when, during the shoots that produced the photo on the previous pages, as well as those here and on the following two pages, John posed with a gun collection, then lit up a cigarette. As for the smoking, J.R. started when he was 12 years old. It was only one of the "bad" things he would do throughout his life. (Hey, he used to eat cotton bolls while working in the fields, despite his mother's warning that they'd cause stomach aches.) On the following pages: John and his boss at Columbia, Goddard Lieberson, conduct a TV interview—yet another example of how celebrities allowed, or at least implied, "total access." There was always a tacit agreement: The media at the time would never, for instance, reveal John's drug use or domestic strife.

SAM PHILLIPS MAY HAVE WANTED ROCKABILLY from Johnny Cash rather than the gospel songs that John brought with him to that first audition at Sun Records, but the artist himself would never eschew the music he had been raised on. Most of the *Personal File* recordings are gospel or gospel-tinged, and, like Elvis, Willie Nelson and George Jones, John dedicated whole albums to nothing but spirituals: *Hymns by Johnny Cash, Hymns from the Heart* (seen here, outtakes from the 1961 photo sessions), *A Believer Sings the Truth, The Gospel Road, The Holy Land.* For this last referenced LP, John traveled to the place in question—Jerusalem and elsewhere in the Middle East—for inspiration and photo opportunities. His fans realize as well that much of his late-in-life American Recordings albums, even before the *Unearthed* box set, comprised either gospel songs written by himself or others (his friend Kris Kristofferson's "Why Me Lord") or rock songs reimagined with completely new neo-gospel settings (U2'S "One," Nine Inch Nails' "Hurt").

FRANK BEZ

ANOTHER OUTTAKE from another photo session from the first half of the '60s, this one for the album *Bitter Tears: Ballads of the American Indian.* John was right for his time, or ours—reverent and, in this instance, politically correct.

JOSE VELAZQUEZ

HE DIDN'T LOVE TO schmooze, but he did what was required. Here, in May of 1962, he glad-hands at a press reception. At this point, folks close to him and those simply listening to the radio are wondering about his career, as the singles and albums aren't steady Top 10s. Even some fine material— "Delia's Gone" and "In the Jailhouse Now," familiar to those who own later discs, both appeared in much earlier versions on 1962's *The Sound of Johnny Cash*—is largely getting lost. John himself is at wits' end, and by 1963 has moved to New York City, leaving his family behind in Southern California.

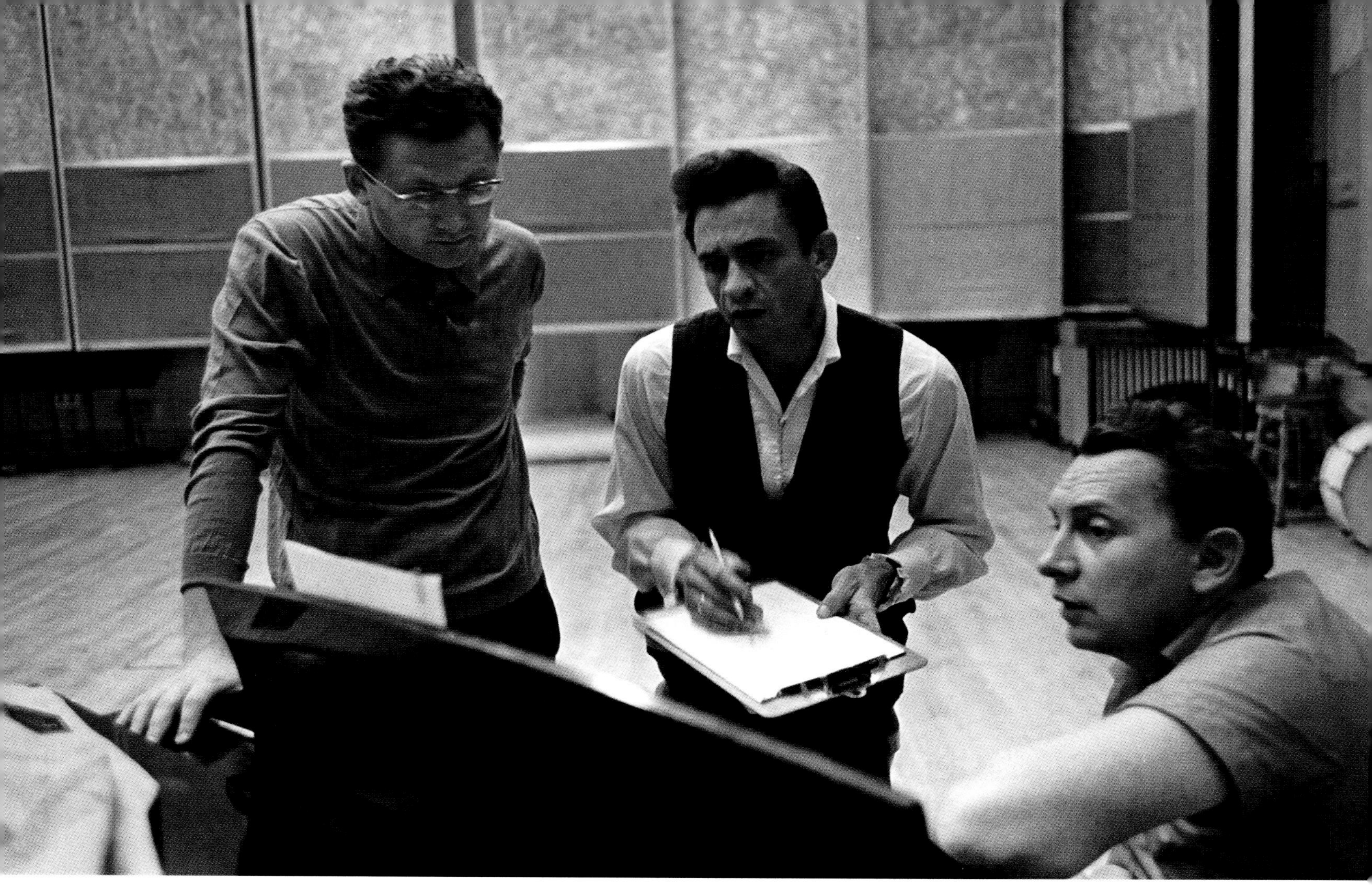

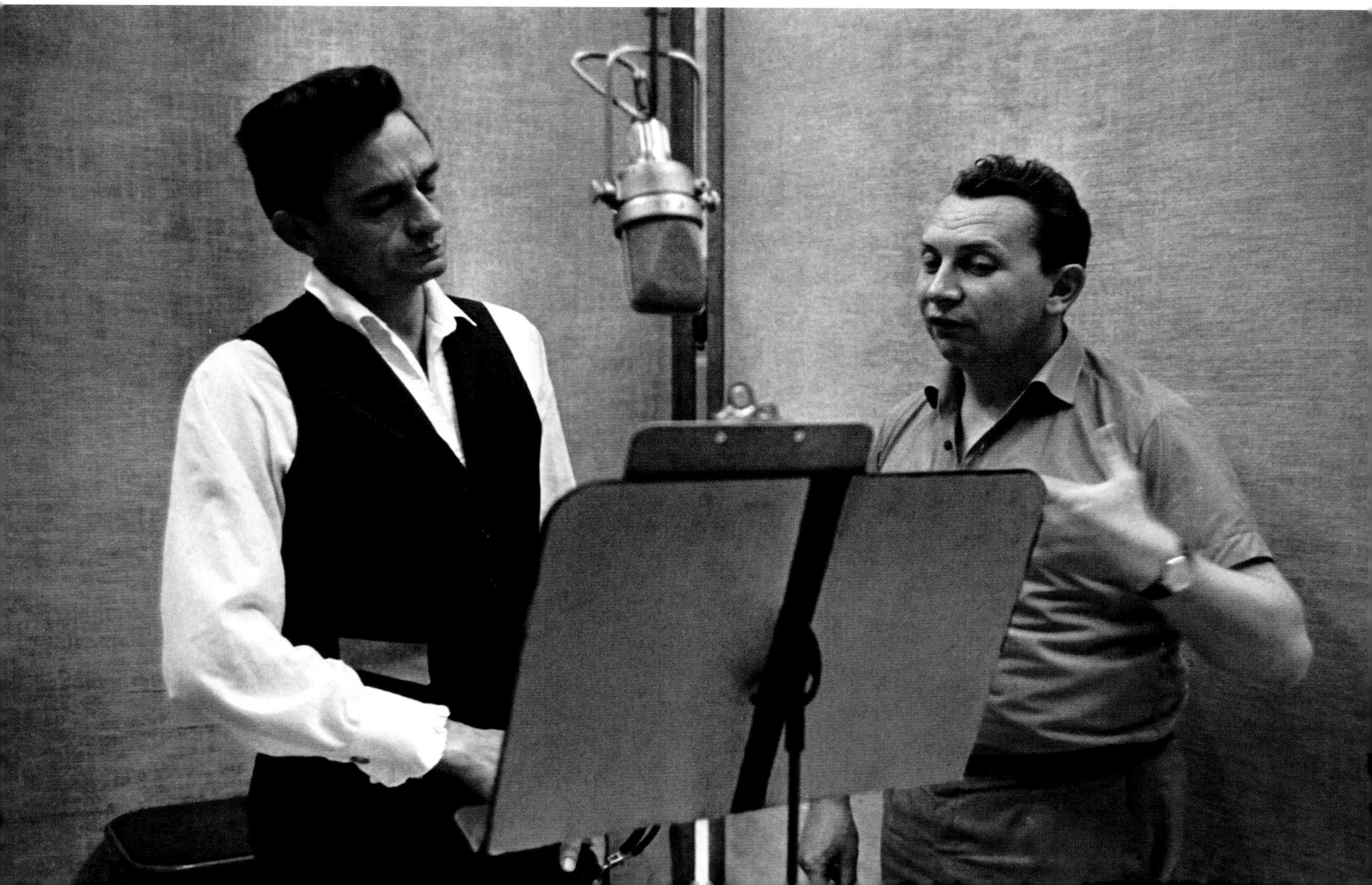

BILL GRINE

IN THE EARLY AND MID-'60s, the nighttime was the wrong time for John, and the nightlife was the bad life: That's when he got in trouble. In 1965 alone he got busted in El Paso that one time for trying to smuggle amphetamines into Texas in his guitar case, and then got himself banned from the Grand Ole Opry after going all ninja on their footlights. In 1966, Vivian would file for divorce. His retreat, as much as he had one, was to spend the days at home (above, in his new house in Hendersonville, Tennessee) or in the studio (opposite and on the following pages, recording the German-language version of "I Walk the Line"). John was deeply experienced by this point and knew how to man the mixing board. But he also kept it simple, and did things as he always had. In fact, Luther Perkins and Marshall Grant were still on guitar and bass in his recording band as well as on the road, just as they had been at the start. The "boom-chicka-boom" sound remained in place.

DON HUNSTEIN (2)

BELIEVE IT OR NOT, even someone as famous as Johnny Cash has obscurities in his oeuvre, and *Mean As Hell!* is certainly one (it's still not available in CD as of 2013). The title refers not (directly) to Johnny's mind-set in mid-1965 when he posed for these possible cover-art photos, but rather to the album's slant: It was a collection of gunfighter and other cowboy ballads, including "The Streets of Laredo," "Bury Me Not on the Lone Prairie," "I Ride an Old Paint" and the title track. The recording stands up fine today, and includes a healthy sampling of something John did as few others would or could: mix evocative spoken-word passages with superb singing. As for whether *Mean As Hell!* left any kind of visual legacy, well, you be the judge. And now we'll move on.

FRANK BEZ (2)

BILL LEVY (3)

JUNE CARTER had continued her own successful singing career both with her family and as a solo artist in the late 1950s and early '60s, while staying in near or distant touch with John. The Carter Family was often on the same bill as Johnny Cash, and June's first husband, the honky-tonk singer Carl Smith, had been a drinking buddy of John's. June had co-written John's megahit "Ring of Fire," which was about, well, everything—her, John, Vivian—and when he and Vivian were calling it quits, June was ready to be more than friends as well, having divorced her second husband, the former football player and car racer Edwin "Rip" Nix, in 1966, after a decade-long marriage. These photos are from a 1967 gig at Shea Stadium, home of the Mets (and hence the souvenir helmet, opposite), in New York City's Queens borough, where John and June shared the stage.

JUNE AND JOHN had a big success together in 1967 with "Jackson," which went to No. 2 on the country charts and was a popular crossover song as well. Early the next year, they were on the road in Canada, and on this particular night the gig was at a place called the Treasure Island Gardens in the city of London, Ontario. John hemmed, hawed, then popped the question onstage in front of some 7,000 or so fans, and he and June were married on March 1, 1968, in Franklin, Kentucky—as we see here. They would be husband and wife for 35 years, until her death in 2003 of complications following heart-valve surgery, quickly followed by his of respiratory complications of diabetes (and complications of a life of bad living, plus complications of a few months on planet Earth without June). That marked the end of the saga of Johnny and June.

John was happy when he hoisted his bride in '68, and happiness indeed prevailed in the early years of the marriage. June helped John cope with his addictions, and he kicked some of them for a goodly while. With June's counsel, John embraced fundamentalist Christianity, a strain of God-worship he had sung about over and over through the years—the years when he was recording professionally and the earlier years when he was harmonizing on spirituals in the fields or in church. This was a major turning point for Cash in 1968—for John the man more than Johnny the entertainer. A turning point or, perhaps, a large red STOP sign. Either way, it was the perfect thing at the time, and he was very happy. So was June.

John's generosity as a performer—and as a star—was made manifest again, even in his relationship with his wife. Although June, as a member of the Carter Family, was folk music royalty, there was no question who had the bigger career as a solo artist, and who should be the family's principal breadwinner, but at every step of the way John made sure that June was by his side—onstage as well as at home (on the next page, they are on tour in England in 1968). They shared the Grammy Award for Best Country & Western Performance Duet, Trio or Group for their 1967 recording of "Jackson," and tore it up with that song on a nightly basis. Their first album together was somewhat provocatively titled *Carryin' On with Johnny Cash & June Carter,* and there were more in the 1970s: *Johnny Cash and His Woman* and *Johnny & June.* When John was in the studio solo (two pages on), June was back home, thoroughly running the show. Upon June's death years later, Rosanne Cash said in a eulogy at the funeral, "If being a wife were a corporation, June would have been a CEO. It was her most treasured role."

MIKE ROUGIER

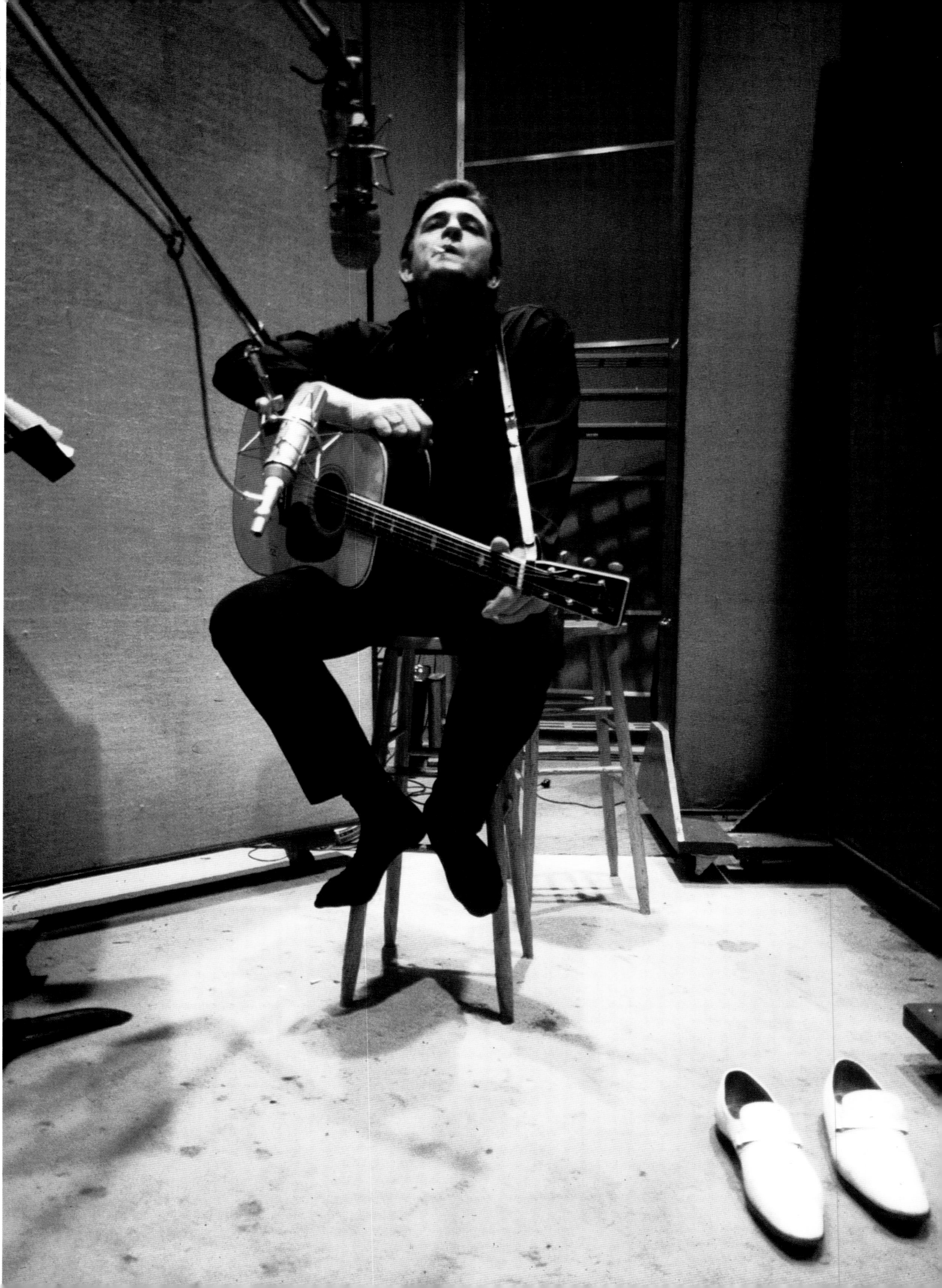

COURTESY JOHN CARTER CASH

AS MIGHT BE EXPECTED,
John, once he had cleaned up, was a better father as well as a better husband and a better companion generally. As mentioned earlier, he and Vivian had four lovely daughters, seen here with Dad (from left: Rosanne, Tara, Cindy and Kathy). June's own two daughters were Rebecca Carlene (who would become the country singer Carlene Carter) and Rosie (who would also become a singer before her accidental death at age 45 by carbon monoxide poisoning, which occurred in 2003: a terrible year for the Carter-Cash clan, which lost June and John at the same time). As the girls graduated from high school, those who chose to do so segued into the family act. Rosanne worked in wardrobe during her dad's tours, then became a backup singer and finally took the occasional solo; Rosie sang backup on her stepfather's TV show. There would be one more singing Carter-Cash to join this Brady Bunch brood, and we will meet him on the pages immediately following.

A SON JOINS six daughters
on March 3, 1970, when John Carter
Cash, John and June's only child
together, is born in Nashville. Here
and on the next two pages, Dad and
Mom—and the nurses and the siblings
at hand—are joyous. John Carter,
as he is known to all who know him,
will grow to be a musician, singer-
songwriter, producer (he has been
involved with numerous Grammy-
winning albums), writer, skilled
outdoorsman and carrier of the family
flame. He first worked as a producer on
his mom's CD *Press On* in 1999,
then assisted Rick Rubin on two of his
dad's American Recordings albums.
He produced his mother's *Wildwood
Flower,* which won the Grammy for Best
Traditional Folk album in 2003, and in
2005 he earned three nominations for
*Unbroken Circle: The Musical Heritage
of the Carter Family.* Meantime,
he wrote children's books and also, in
2007, a memoir: *Anchored in Love:
An Intimate Portrait of June Carter Cash.*
In the pages ahead, we will revisit
some of what John Carter wrote about
in that book, but let it suffice for now:
It was difficult to recount a sometimes
wonderful, sometimes harrowing
upbringing. His parents loved one
another unconditionally, John Carter has
said and written, but there were fights,
there was the hovering fear of divorce (at
least, as sensed by their children),
and there was the constant specter of
addiction, which eventually visited June
as well as John. In 1970, however—
with a healthy baby boy and Johnny
Cash as big a star as ever, with his
television show a major hit—everything
was coming up roses.

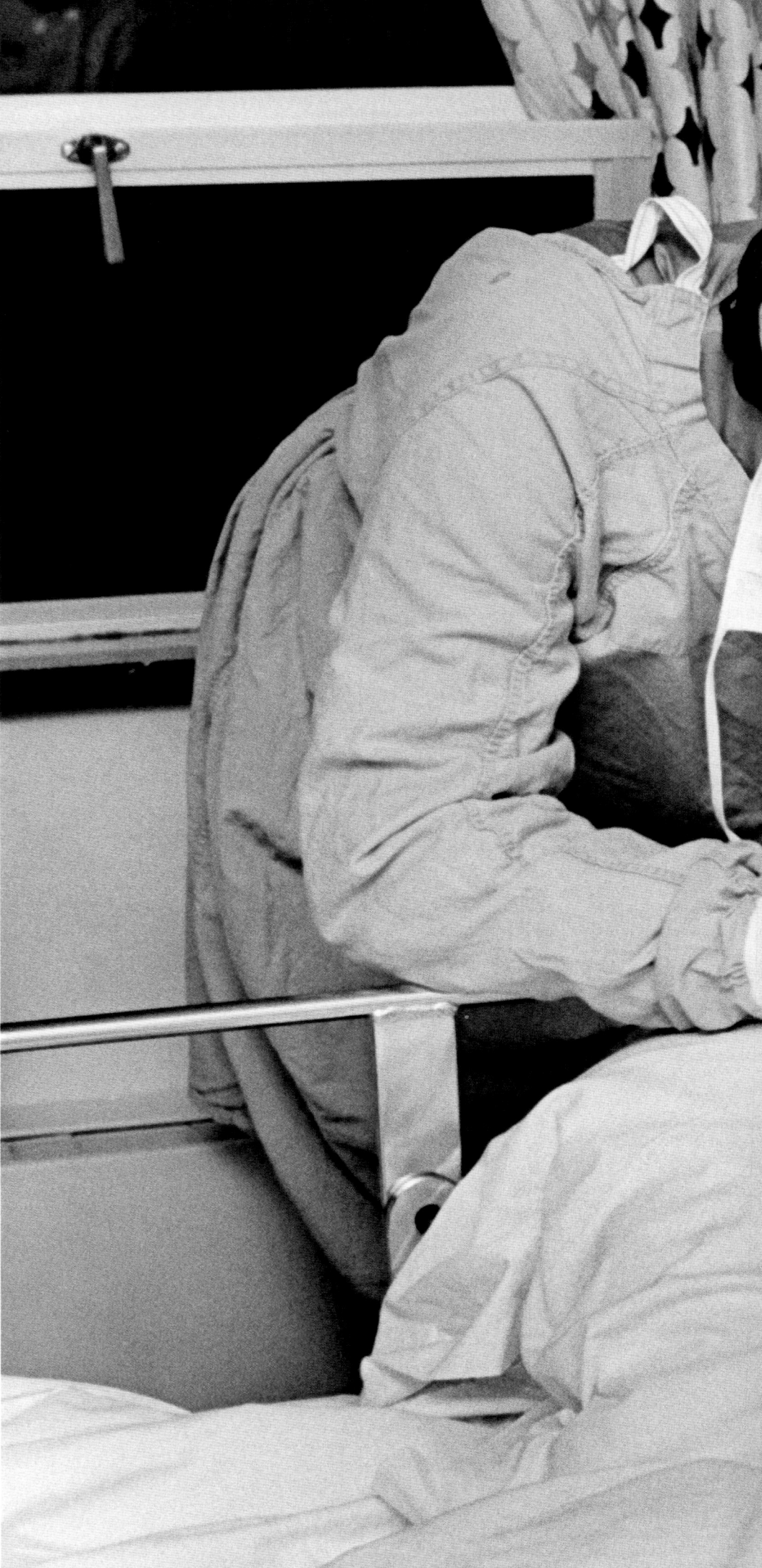

J.T. PHILLIPS

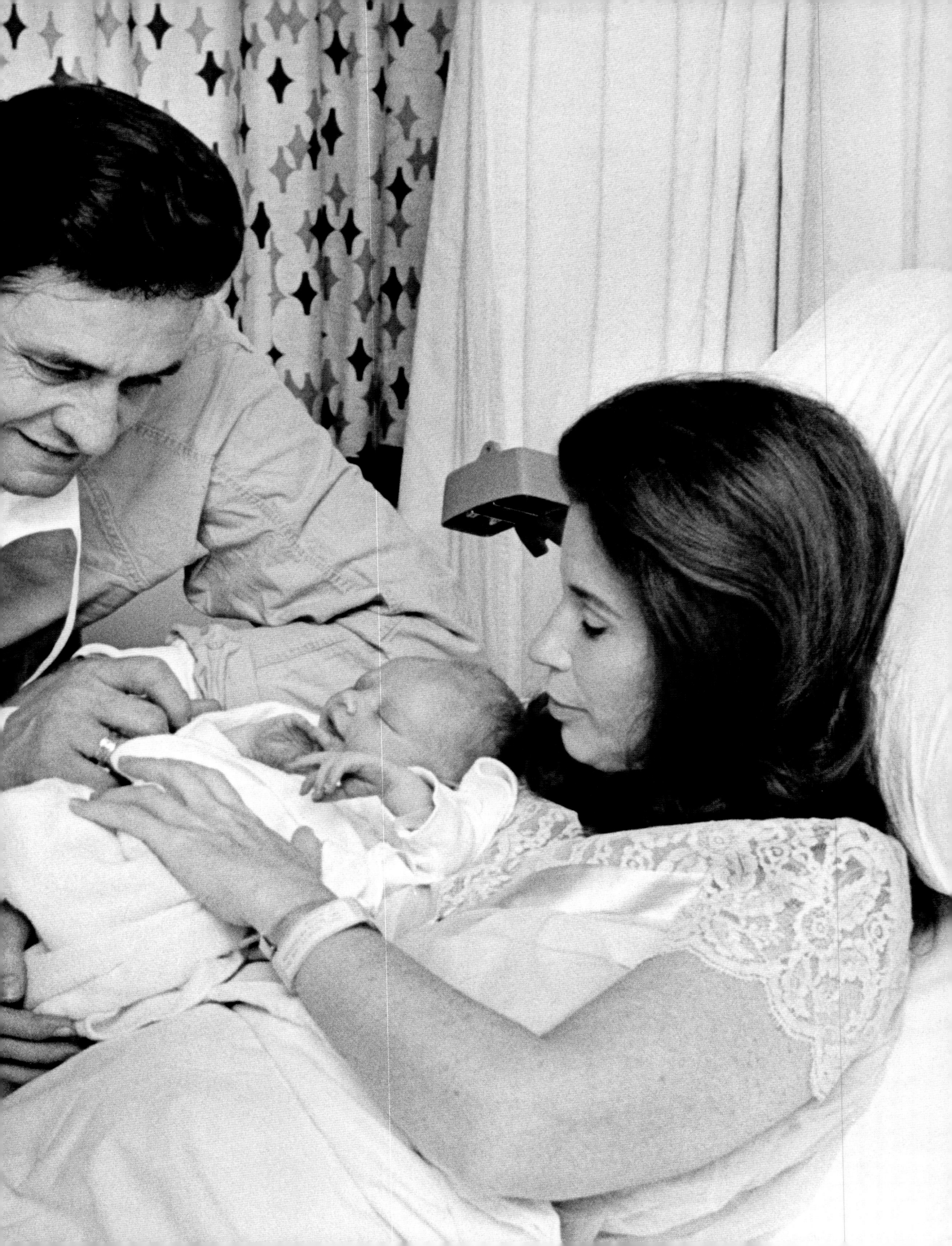

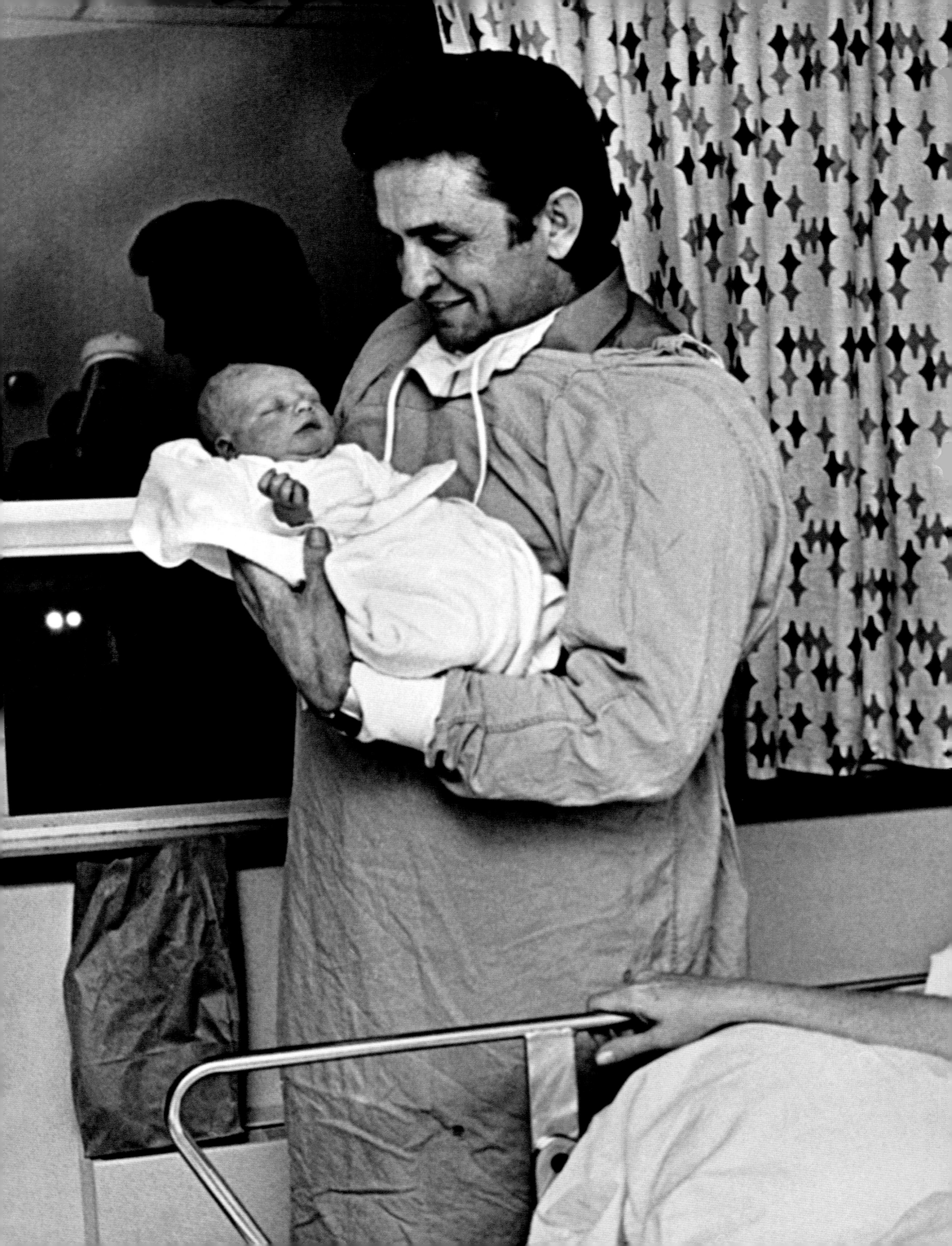

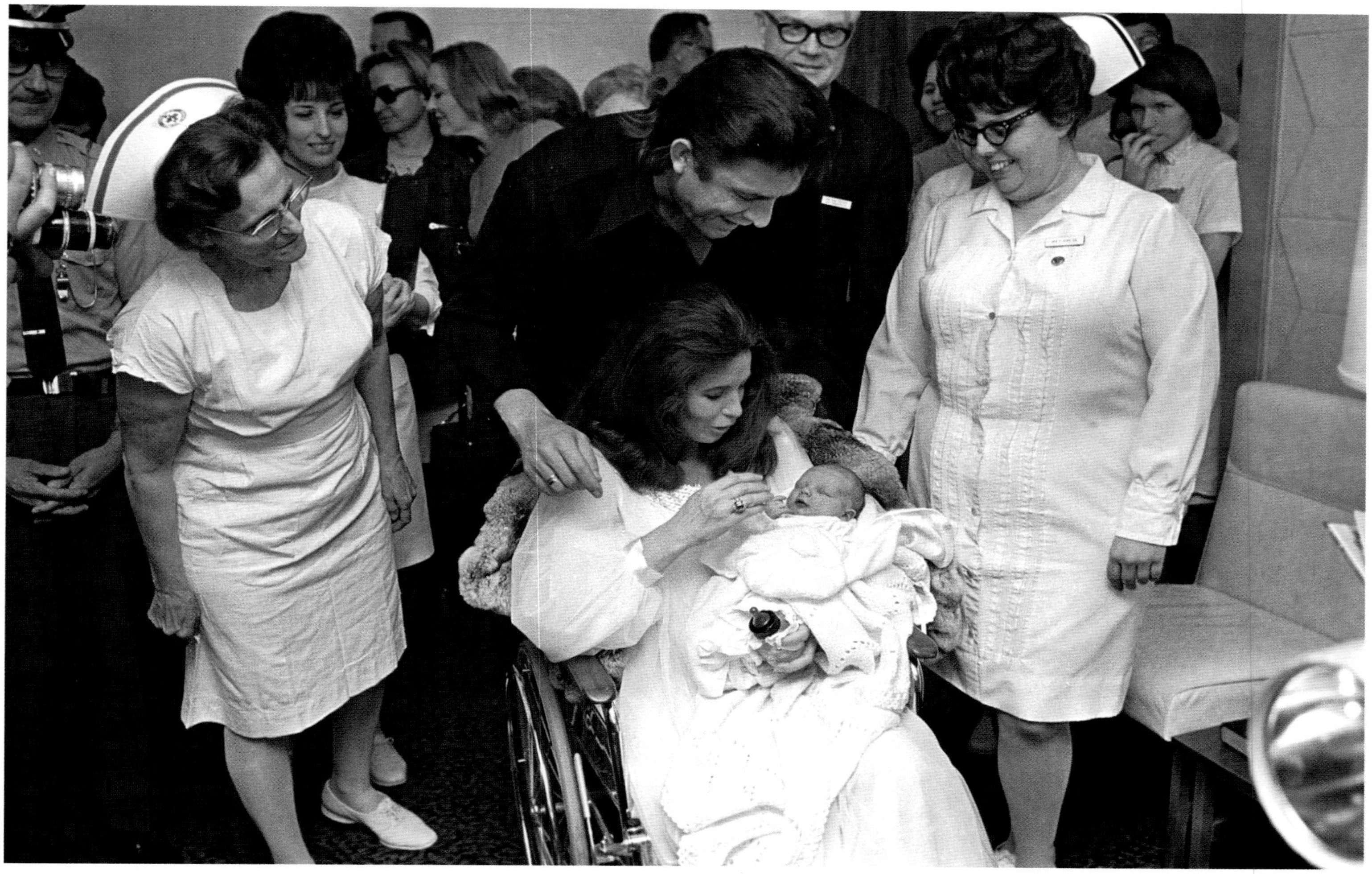

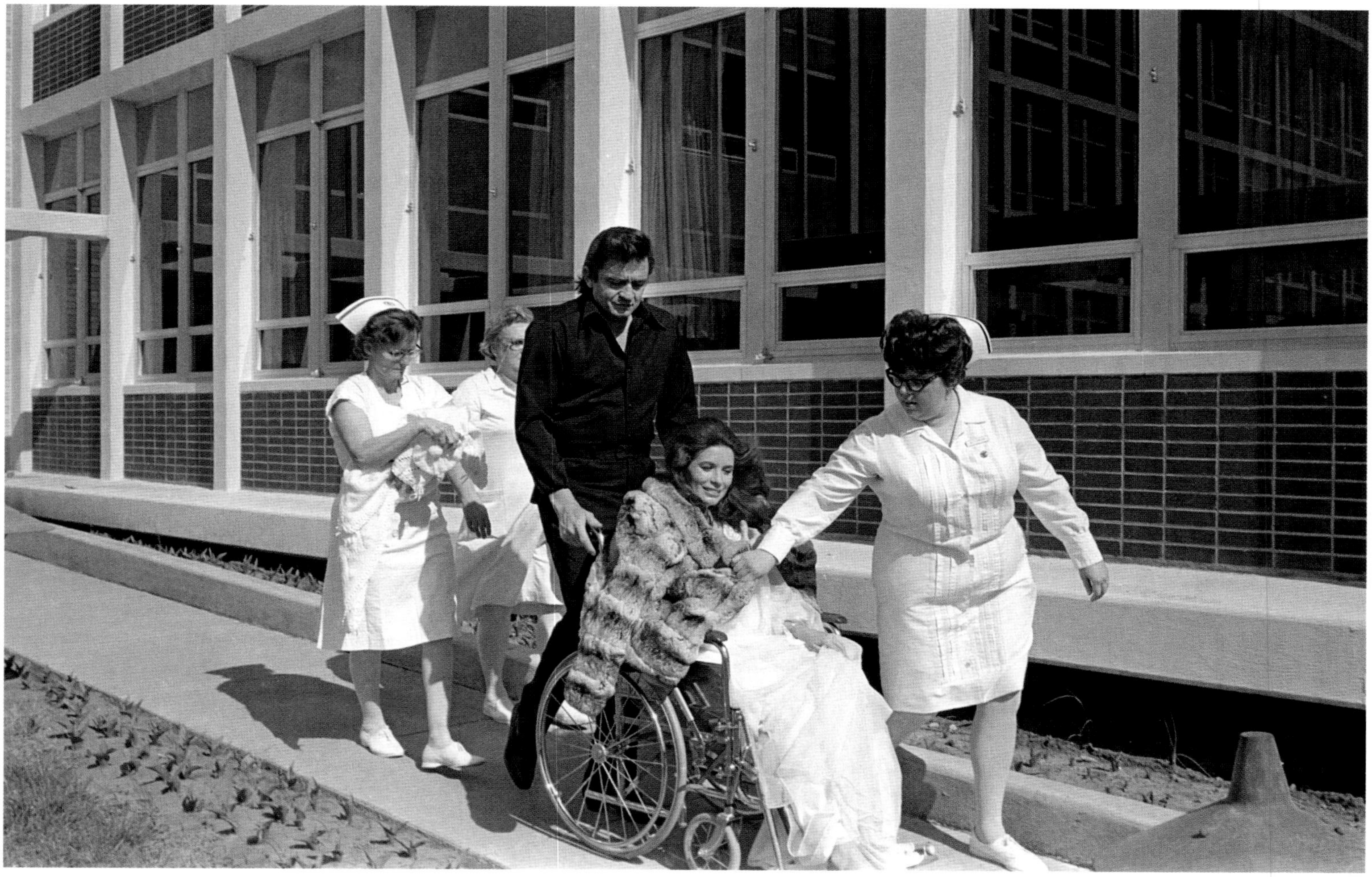

J.T. PHILLIPS (3)

"**WELL, I MISS** the sounds of Tennessee," Rosanne Cash wrote and sang, in a song she composed after her father died in 2003, "and the smell of heavy rain / The roses in the garden / Laugh before the pain/ But I hear his voice close in my ear / I see her smile and wave / I blink and while my eyes are closed / They both have gone away." In the chorus: "Blue bare room, the wood and nails / There's nothing left to take / But love and years are not for sale / In our old house on the lake . . ."

THE HOUSE ON THE
LAKE

BOB CATO

THE HOUSE had a prosaic address— 200 Caudill Drive in Hendersonville, Tennessee—but a poetic aspect in its beautiful expanse, its rough-hewn situation and all the human drama enacted there through the years. It wasn't so much on Caudill Drive as it was on Old Hickory Lake, and after California and New York it was the place John came home to, to live with June and all sorts of children and eventually grandchildren. It was the home that J.R. Cash had always sought and always, after the flood of fame, needed. The motto on the Cash family coat of arms reads "Better Times Will Come," and in John's way of thinking: That could have been the motto of the lake house.

It is obvious to its fans that we haven't yet mentioned *Walk the Line,* the fine biographical film—we haven't played off it, said where it might have been right, where it was a little bit wrong. That has been purposeful; John's life was very much more complicated than those two hours could capture. Nor could any narrative we might write do justice in 192 pages. So we have decided to let these pictures speak largely for themselves. That said, anyone who has seen the film and now looks at the photographs on the next 20 pages must remark: The movie sure got that right. It did. As deft as the performances were—and we should note that June and John (shortly before they died) approved Reese Witherspoon and Joaquin Phoenix as the leads—the film was even more faithful to the lake house in Hendersonville and rightly suggested how much that property meant to John. The house itself was featured in the film, and some of its rooms, circa the period in question, were painstakingly recreated in constructed sets.

John bought the house in the late '60s, not realizing that he was on the verge of a second wave of superstardom, this one thanks to that great American nation-mover-and-shaker, television. When *The Johnny Cash Show,* broadcast from down the road at the Ryman Auditorium (Hendersonville is 18 miles northeast of downtown Nashville), caught on with a national audience, the lake house became not only a retreat from fame but, as we shall see, something of a clubhouse for John's latest generation of pals.

JOHN WOULD OWN OTHER
places, even unto Jamaica, but
Hendersonville was where he could
relax, as can be seen on these next eight
pages. With its natural setting, near
where Roy Orbison had a place, this
was quite a spread, stretching along
the rocky shoreline of Old Hickory
Lake. Outdoors, there was a swimming
pool and a bell garden, but the charm
of the woodland near the water was
an attraction best left unspoiled. The
house itself was a rustic mansion:
a 13,880-square-foot rambling edifice
built on a solid rock foundation.
A highlight consisted of a number of
immense 35-foot-diameter rooms, and
there were seven bedrooms and five
full bathrooms. The house was filled
with hand-carved, dark wood furniture
that the Cashes found during their
global travels—John and June were
both big shoppers and prone to the
extravagant gesture, which sometimes
caused financial problems—and the
walls featured portraits of family
members and close friends such as
Waylon Jennings and Carl Perkins. One
table supported a collection of acoustic
instruments once played by the original
Carter Family. There were also framed
gold records, of course, but the one
for "I Walk the Line" was hung at
a smaller ranch house across the street
at 185 Caudill Drive, and therein lies
another story. This was called Mama
Cash's House, and indeed was where
John's mother lived in her last years.
(She pitched in by working at the House
of Cash museum in Hendersonville,
downtown in the building where the
family's business affairs were also
centered.) John, too, lived his very last
days at the ranch house, when getting
around the lake house in his wheelchair
proved problematical.

HAPPINESS was more easily attained in Hendersonville than elsewhere, and certainly in this series of pictures and in the photograph on the next two pages, John and June are happy at the lake house. It should be added: According to John Carter Cash's 2007 book on his mother, happiness was more general in the 1970s than the '80s, when a slump in his father's career caused financial difficulties and his parents were forced to sell jewelry and other possessions to pay their sizable domestic staff. But earlier, when John's variety show was going strong, the lake house was the center of a rolling party, and June, who ran the place, was the perfect hostess. Eventually, John and some of his musical friends would make their way through a hallway and down some stairs to the lakeside room where they would engage in their legendary "guitar pulls." John remembered to LIFE in 1994: "In 1968, '69, when I was doing my TV show, we'd invite singers and guitar players over for dinner. Afterward, everyone had to take the hot seat and do at least two songs. The most memorable night was in '69. Kris Kristofferson sang 'Me and Bobby McGee,' Bob Dylan sang 'Lay Lady Lay,' Joni Mitchell sang 'Both Sides Now,' Graham Nash sang 'Marrakesh Express,' and Shel Silverstein sang 'A Boy Named Sue'—all in the same night. People had never heard those songs, and the very next week, when I played San Quentin prison, I took 'A Boy Named Sue' with me."

J.T. PHILLIPS (3)

FOR A YOUNG BOY, the lake house was heaven, and surely life in Hendersonville nurtured John Carter's love of the outdoors. "The house was large, but it was home, and never felt stuffy or empty," he says today. Here he plays with the dog and is attended by nurse Winifred Kelly, and visits with Grandma and Grandpa Cash and their bird (top). In his memoir, John Carter said that as he grew older he became aware of tensions in his parents' marriage, and, later still, of their addictions—John relapsing in the 1980s and '90s, June becoming reliant on prescription drugs.

JOHN CARTER, seen here
helping Daddy drive on the property,
remembered that when he was a
child, he cried as he heard his parents
fight for hours one day. He wrote that
the arguments between the two never
became physical, but that he heard
his mother threaten to leave the family.
He lived in fear that his parents would
divorce. That one day must have been
the worst, because he remembered
it best: The parents argued and argued,
and eventually became aware that
their boy must have been a witness.
Finally, they called to John Carter and
said they had to deliver some news.
He held his breath, expecting to hear
that the family was coming apart.
Instead, they told him they had decided
to renew their marriage vows—which
they did do. In promoting his book,
which was published four years after
his parents' deaths, John Carter said
they would have wanted him to write
it, because they always chose to be
honest about life—the good and the
bad. John Carter now looks back,
10 years after his parents' deaths, and
sums up: "My mother and father had
a love like none other. Though there
were rough times, the strength of their
relationship endured. When my mother
and father came together, onstage
or off, something special happened. My
mother had a way of softening the Man
in Black. Somehow he was more tender
by her side. Gentler." The ballad of
John and June was a true country song,
more real than any lyric.

J.T. PHILLIPS

WHENEVER THERE WAS a guitar handy, music might fill any room in the lake house—and there was always a guitar handy. Here, Roy Orbison takes his turn on the hot seat before an intimate audience that includes (from left) Johnny; Braxton Dixon, who built the lake house, and his wife, Anna; Kris Kristofferson, with two women close by; June, in the shadows; and Jack Palance. After both June and John died, four months apart, the lake house was sold by John Carter to the British singer Barry Gibb and his wife. The former Bee Gees star said he intended to renovate, but he promised to keep the house true to its heritage and preserve it as a place of homage to Johnny Cash. As they were planning the remodeling in 2007, the house caught fire and burned to its foundations. Famous neighbors gathered, many of whom had close connections to John, June and the house itself. "So many prominent things and prominent people in American history took place in that house," said the singer Marty Stuart, who lived right next door and had been married to John's daughter Cindy in the 1980s. "Everyone from Billy Graham to Bob Dylan went into that house." He added that for John, the house had been "a sanctuary and a fortress." Said another Caudill Drive neighbor, Richard Sterban of the Oak Ridge Boys, a group that had been helped at regular intervals by John: "Maybe it's the good Lord's way to make sure that it was only Johnny's house."

AS A JAILBIRD, John was a fly-by-night visitor, never in for the long haul. He had the reputation of being an hombre toughened by hard experience in stir, but this is legend, not fact. He was never in state or federal prison except to sing songs there, and spent a grand total of seven nights in jail for various offenses through the years. The most violence he encountered in custody was probably when, after being arrested for public drunkenness in Starkville, Mississippi, he broke his toe by kicking the bars of his cell. But as for playing to prisoners and lifting their spirits: Well, he was the Bob Hope of the behind-bars circuit.

THE PRISON
CONCERTS

FOLSOM PRISON, where John is sitting before his performance for the convicts in 1968, and San Quentin were the two famous "prison concerts," but that's entirely because they were recorded. There were many others, some much earlier than the well-known late-'60s shows.

For reasons probably linked to his personal sense of empathy, John was always drawn to prisoners. He first became aware of Folsom State Prison in Sacramento County, California, when he was in the Air Force and, in 1953, was shown a documentary film, *Inside the Walls of Folsom Prison.* Cash was moved to write "Folsom Prison Blues," and that became the A-side of his second single for Sun Records. Inmates heard it, took to it, and some of them started corresponding with the singer. The bolder of them asked if he might perform at their institutions, and in 1957, Cash sang at the state penitentiary in Huntsville, Texas. News spread on the inmate grapevine that the show, filled with songs of trial and hardship as well as fun, novelty numbers, had been terrific. "The word got around among the convicts that I was one of them, because of the songs I sang," John told LIFE. "So I started getting a lot of requests for prison concerts and started doing a lot of them. I first did San Quentin prison [in California's Marin County] in, I think, 1958. Merle Haggard can tell you the date. He was in the audience."

(Haggard was authentically hardened in a way Cash was not: Busted for attempted robbery in 1957, he spent two years and nine months in San Quentin, where he ran a gambling and bootlegging operation out of his cell. He later said that the Johnny Cash concert inspired him to join the prison band, and of course the rest of that is history—and a different book.)

John went on from San Quentin to many other prison shows through the years, and by 1967 he realized that these concerts might be worth capturing on record. He pitched the idea, and Columbia execs took it to officials at San Quentin and Folsom. The folks at Folsom quickly said yes, and on January 10, 1968, John and June and John's father, Ray, checked into the El Rancho Motel in Sacramento. June and others who would perform at the show—a roster that included Carl Perkins and the Statler Brothers—are seen at Folsom on the following pages, waiting to take the stage for a gig like no other.

© JIM MARSHALL PHOTOGRAPHY LLC

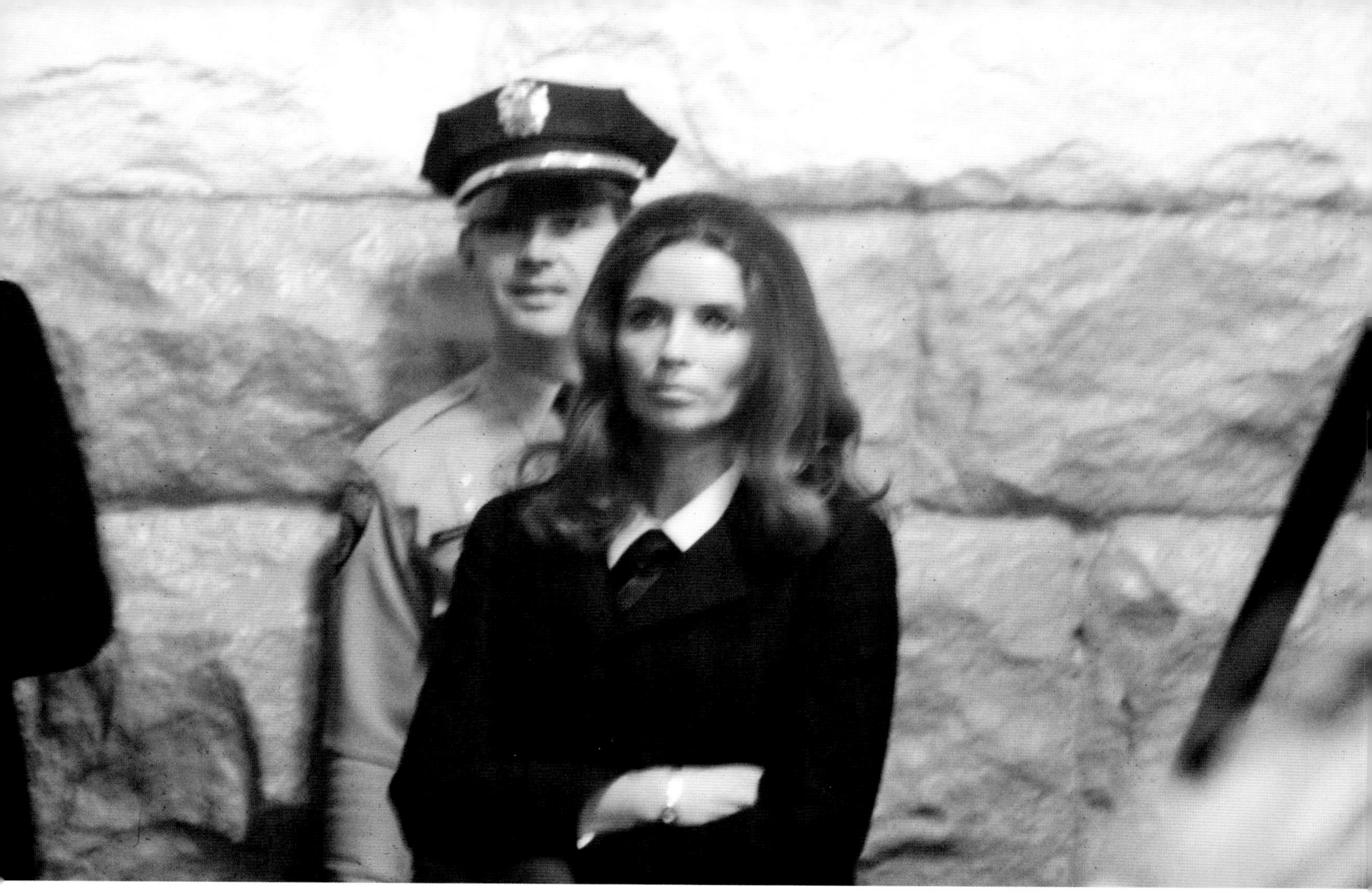

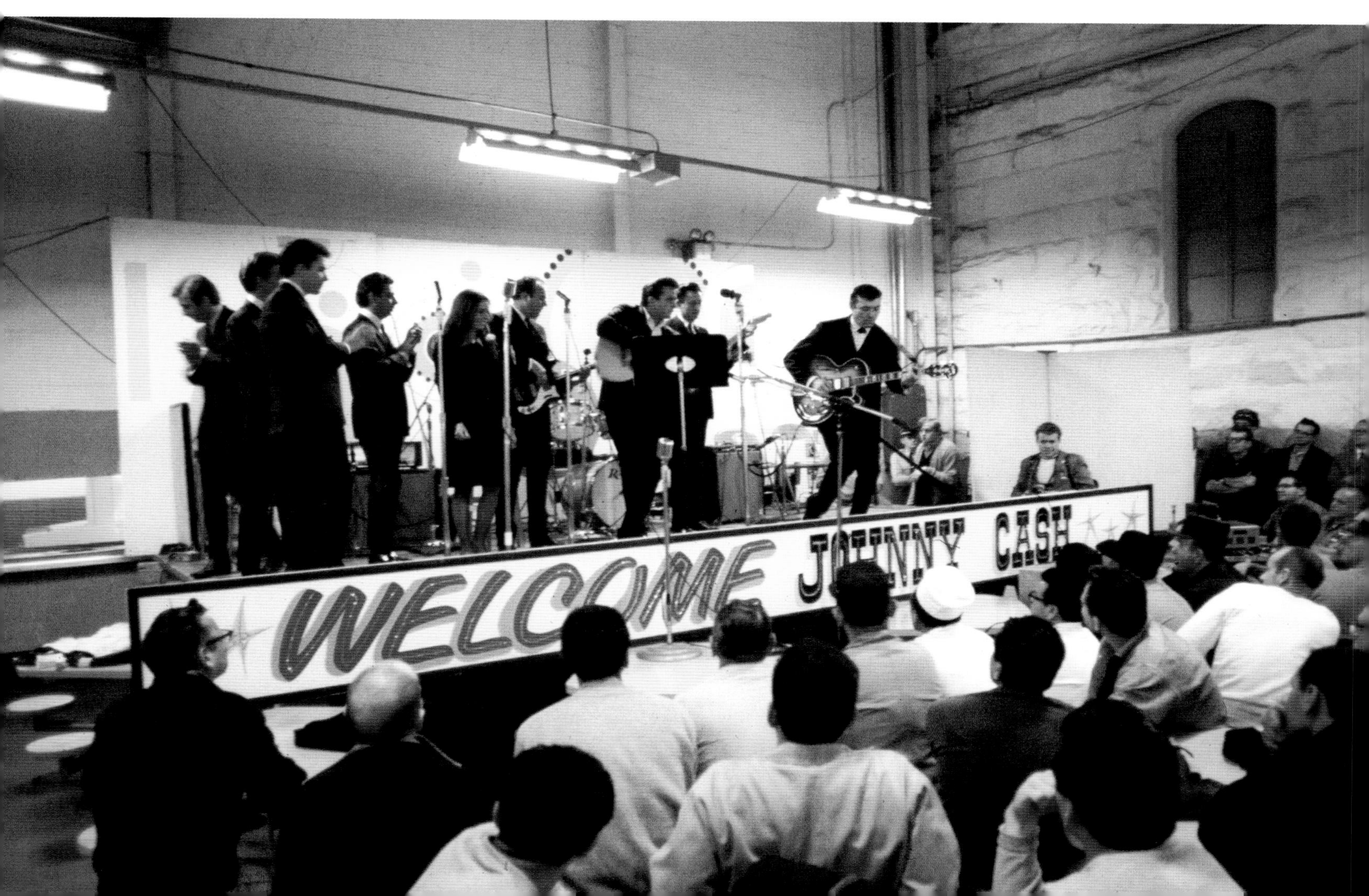
WELCOME JOHNNY CASH

JUNE WASN'T TENSE but was properly sober-minded at the prison, as was everybody. Yet once the concert began (after two days of rehearsals and an inspiring visit by California governor Ronald Reagan, who happened to also be at the El Rancho), the bandmates and inmates all had a ball—as can be seen here and on the following pages. The first show was slated for 9:40 a.m. and the second for 12:40 p.m. on January 13, and the program included Perkins singing "Blue Suede Shoes," the Statler Brothers doing "Flowers on the Wall" and Cash performing, among other selections, prison songs such as "The Wall" and (of course) "Folsom Prison Blues," plus yuck-it-up numbers like "Dirty Old Egg-Sucking Dog" (today, the background music for a Volkswagen Jetta TV commercial). A highlight of the concert was a song written by Glen Sherley, an inmate, and that story will be told just a few pages on.

JOHN PRAYS in the prison chapel during downtime. His thoughts are surely with the inmates, and perhaps he focuses on Glen Sherley—the subject of one of the most fascinating stories in Johnny Cash lore. Incarcerated for armed robbery, Sherley was also a man of musical talent. He had written and sung a song and had given it to the Reverend Floyd Gressett, a Ventura priest who regularly visited Folsom. John picked up the story from there when talking with LIFE: "The night before I was going to record at Folsom prison, I got to the motel and a preacher friend of mine brought me a tape of a song called 'Greystone Chapel.' He said a convict had written it about the chapel at Folsom. I listened to it one time and I said, 'I've got to do this in the show tomorrow.' So I stayed up and learned it, and the next day the preacher had him in the front row. I announced, 'This song was written by Glen Sherley.' It was a terrible, terrible thing to point him out among all those cons, but I didn't think about that then. Everybody just had a fit, screaming and carrying on. After a year or so, he was paroled. He did an album, a good one, and he wrote 'Portrait of My Woman,' which Eddy Arnold had a hit record off of. [What happened to Sherley], there are two stories, and I don't know enough to tell you which one to believe. It was either suicide or cancer—I know there was a gun involved. The last time I saw him, he was back in California, working for some big cattle company, feeding 10,000 cattle a day. He lived in the cab of a semi truck. He didn't want any more of public life. Just couldn't handle it." For the record: Glen Sherley died in California on May 11, 1978, from a self-inflicted gunshot wound to the head.

JOHN HAD BEEN DOWN in the dumps before he suggested a prison record to Columbia: The TV show hadn't debuted yet, and sales had progressively slowed during the 1960s. He thought that the memorable shows he was putting on behind prison walls deserved to be commemorated, but hoped as well that such a unique record release might help him out of this particular commercial slump. Now, the performances done, he knew he had been right about the first part—knew it as soon as he packed up his guitar case at Folsom. As for the second part, *At Folsom Prison,* released in May of 1968, just four months after it had been recorded, was an instant hit: No. 1 on the country charts, No. 13 on the *Billboard* national-album chart, with the lead single, the live version of "Folsom Prison Blues," affording John his first Top 40 hit in four years. The album has by now gone three times platinum, and back then it of course spawned a sequel, *At San Quentin,* which was an even bigger success. John's fourth visit to that other California prison produced, within a year, a TV special for Granada in Great Britain and this second killer record, which not only went No. 1 country in the U.S. but also was No. 1 for four weeks on the *Billboard* 200 and spun off the unstoppable single "A Boy Named Sue" (barely a week off the guitar strings of Shel Silverstein; please see page 109), which, in an AM version with a couple of profanities bleeped out, climbed to No. 1 on the country charts and No. 2 on the Hot 100 chart. That song, by the way, is hardly a "novelty." Listen to it again. It's a terrific invention, a wonderful story-song, and is brought home by yet another perfect Johnny Cash vocal.

AT SAN QUENTIN, John knew full well that the audio tapes were rolling and that Granada TV was filming—he even informed the inmates: "I tell you what, the show is being recorded and televised for . . . England!" He said that he had been coached to turn this way and that, sing this particular song and that one. "I just don't get it, man!" he complained to loud applause. He said that he was here to do "what you want me to, and what I want to do! So what do you want to hear?" The requests poured forth in a torrent. Johnny Cash raised his guitar to his chin and launched into such songs as "I Walk the Line." In the photos on this page are Johnny and Carl Perkins (top) and Tommy Cash harmonizing with his brother (above).

THIS SAN QUENTIN
photograph, chosen for every good
reason for the Columbia album cover,
is another of our signature pictures
that, even in a book of rarities, is a
required inclusion. Any volume aspiring
to tell the Johnny Cash story needs
the Million Dollar Quartet moment, and
needs this strong image from 1969. It
captures the singer about to reemerge,
big-time, in the spotlight. His TV show
is on the horizon and now there's this
album; in the coming months they
will combine to push each other to
higher heights. We at LIFE thought that
Johnny Cash fans would want the
At San Quentin photograph without the
type on it. In that way, at least, it is
a rarity. As for Cash's prison concerts:
They were hardly done. He not only
continued to perform before inmates,
he became even more of an activist for
prison reform. On July 26, 1972, he
was introduced by Tennessee senator
William Brock to the U.S. Senate
Subcommittee addressing the issue,
and told them that inmates needed,
almost above all else, a modicum of
hope. Less than three months later,
John gave his first free jailhouse concert
outside the U.S., at Österåker Prison
just north of Stockholm, Sweden.
So here's a trivia answer: The concert
was recorded, and *Johnny Cash på
Österåker* is not only John's third great
prison-concert LP, but—if you can find
it in vinyl—a true rarity among rarities.

THE ~~I~~
BLA~~

JOHNNY CASH WAS STILL
a stranger to a substantial part of
American audience as late as the
summer of 1969—it's a fact. He h
had the country hits, but that didn
it for certain segments of our postw
society. Some folks revered him as
a god, some folks didn't know him
from Adam. That was about to cha
because he was about to turn arou
melodramatically, look the TV cam
square in the eye and sonorously
intone, for the ten thousandth time
and for the edification of those he w
meeting for the first time ever, "Hel
I'm Johnny Cash."

NOTHING ELSE has the capacity to bolster—even cement—a celebrity's public image in the American mind-set like exposure on national television. We perhaps had heard those yeah-yeah Beatles sounds on the radio in early 1964, but then we saw them on *The Ed Sullivan Show* and, wow, that was something else. We knew Michael Jackson had grown up some and was no longer the cute little kid singing with his brothers, but then he moonwalked before our eyes on the Motown 25th Anniversary special, and the next morning at the water cooler there was nothing else to be discussed. Madonna was arguably a child of MTV as much as of radio.

Johnny Cash had been playing with the black-clothes thing for a while; if you flip through the pages of this book you see him growing darker year by year, and by the time he's appearing for the cons and the cameras at Folsom and San Quentin he's got the look locked and loaded. His sound had been set in stone for a while, and was formidable. It's worthwhile to pause here and note: It wasn't a strictly country sound. It wasn't the least bit twangy or high lonesome— beautiful sounds, to be sure, but off-putting to some northern ears. It was bottomless in its bass and altogether different. He sang folk songs as often as he sang country songs, and when he went up-tempo it was always rockabilly, which is to say rock 'n' roll. In his autobiography, *Cash,* he wrote that if he were stranded on a desert island, the recordings he would need would include *The Freewheelin' Bob Dylan,* Merle Travis's *Down Home,* a compilation of Jimmie Davis's greatest gospel hits, Emmylou Harris's *Roses in the Snow,* Rosanne Cash's *The Wheel,* any gospel collection by Sister Rosetta Tharpe, "something by Beethoven" and a selection of *You Are There* radio broadcasts. There you have it!

So one Saturday night after dinner in the summer of '69, America turns the dial—there were no remotes back then, children—and America sees there's an off-season replacement show for *The Hollywood Palace,* its beloved variety hour. Suddenly this severe-looking oily-haired man is staring at them, and even though he's saying "Hello," he seems a bit menacing. Then he starts to sing, which has always had a way of mesmerizing folks. And then he proceeds to unwrap one of the strangest, most wonderful, most ecumenical American entertainment packages ever to grace the small screen. *The Johnny Cash Show* would only last a few seasons and, despite how fondly it is remembered, and despite the fact that in the who-wants-to-watch-TV? days of summer it reached No. 1 once or twice, it wasn't really a reliable Top 10 show (17th for the complete 1970 season). But it was vastly influential because it reached across all sorts of fences in the severely picketed America of 1969 and '70, and offered to shake a hand. The guest lists and set lists—as well as the pictures—that will be reviewed on the next several pages are scarcely to be believed, even all these years later. John left a number of great legacies, personal and professional. This was one, and it cut both ways. It was professional, but even more: It was personal.

THE GRACIOUS HOST smiles lovingly at his lovely guest, the coal-miner's daughter herself, Loretta Lynn, who this night sings "I Know How." Lynn was country royalty, of course, but many of John's guests were otherwise. The first show featured not only a number of those who would be weekly regulars—John, June, his Tennessee Three, her Carter kinfolk, Carl Perkins and the Statler Brothers—but also Bob Dylan, Joni Mitchell and the Cajun fiddler Doug Kershaw, plus the comic Fannie Flagg. "Well, it was the No. 1 show for a while," John told LIFE in 1994. "Of course, when we first talked about doing it, I heard grumblings. 'We're not going to have so-and-so on this show in Nashville.' And I heard Pete Seeger's name mentioned." (The folksinger Seeger had essentially been blacklisted from television for his liberal politics, specifically his anti–Vietnam War stance that had caused a brouhaha on a rival network.) "Pete's a friend of mine. I've sat in his cabin in New York and played rhythm while he played fretless banjo for many hours. So I told them, 'If I do a weekly show, I insist on Pete Seeger being one of my guests, as well as Bob Dylan, if I can get them.' There was grumbling, there were heads huddled, and finally I had to say, 'It's either my way or the highway. I'm gone.' So they went for it. They thought they were 'closely monitoring' everything Pete Seeger did. But it turned out he was just a folksinger with a banjo—which, by the way, worked really good on the show—and how much can you monitor a folksinger with a banjo?"

J.T. PHILLIPS

TO KEEP THE PEACE with the network and with many thousands of viewers, John welcomed such as Bob Hope (middle row, right), Burl Ives and Peggy Lee to the stage, but also Linda Ronstadt, Kris Kristofferson, Neil Young, Gordon Lightfoot and James Taylor. Merle Haggard and Tammy Wynette were guests, of course, and so were the Cowsills and the Monkees—of course. In the gallery above, clockwise from bottom left, we see Brenda Lee, O.C. Smith, Ricky Nelson, Mama Cass Elliot, Hope and the Everly Brothers. And on the opposite page are two iconic American folksingers: Judy Collins (top) and, on the very first program, Bob Dylan. For those who liked it, this was the greatest show on earth.

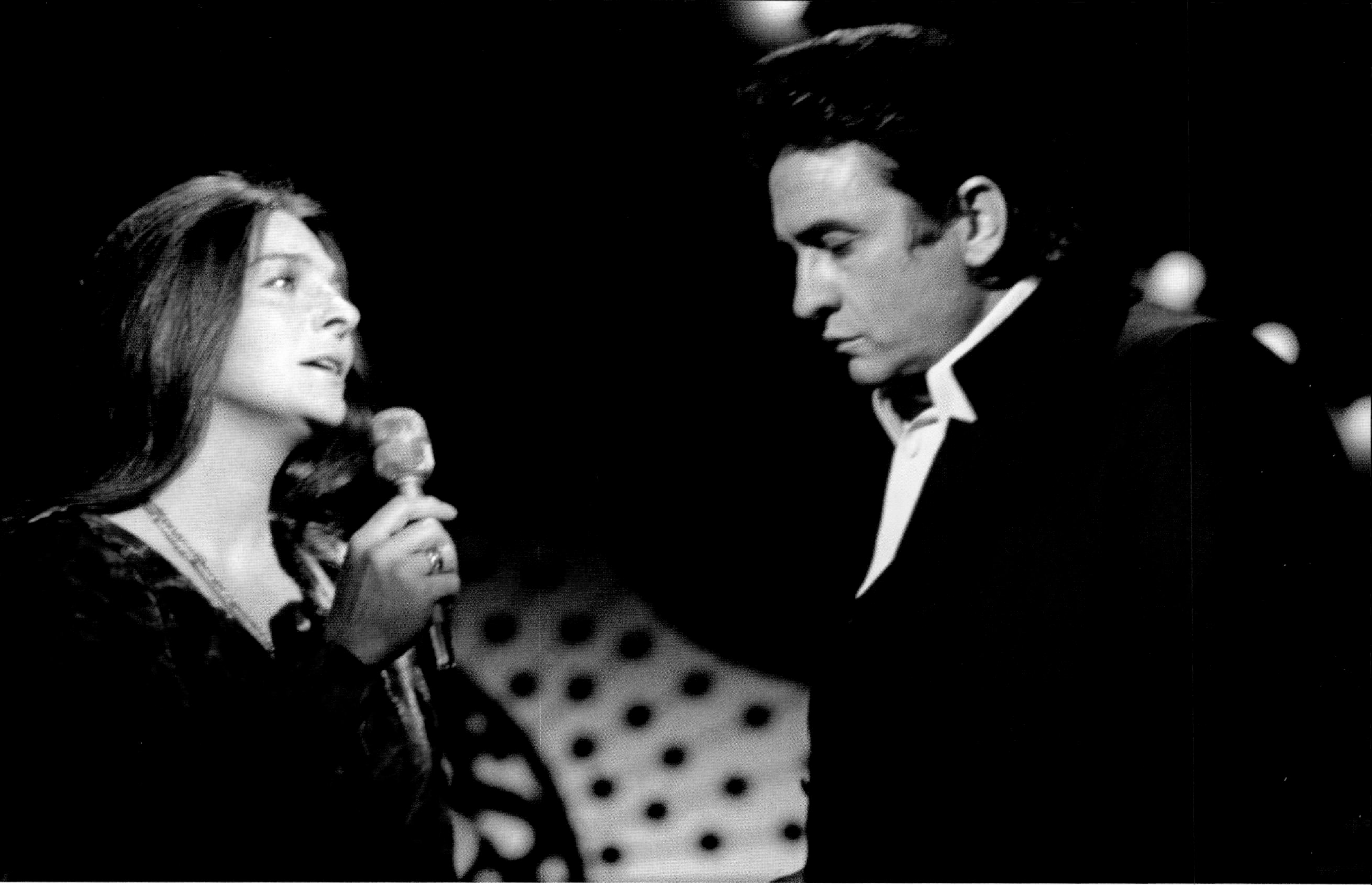

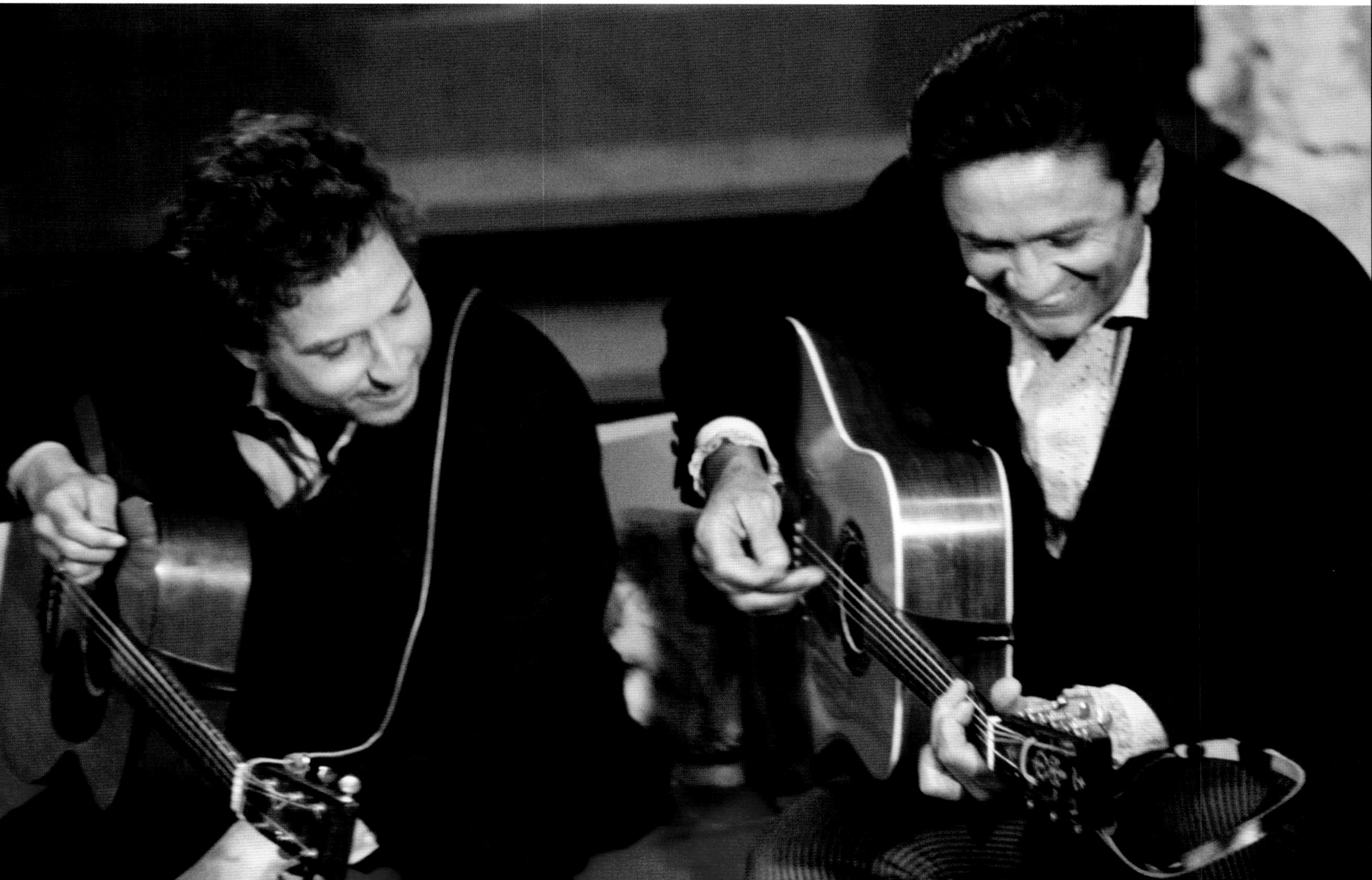

WE COULD GO ON and on with this, it's so much fun. Episode 18 of *The Johnny Cash Show* featured the wonderful blue-eyed soul singer Dusty Springfield, the bathetic poet/sorta-singer Rod McKuen and for some reason Kirk Douglas. The next week the musical guests were titans from several genres: Ray Charles, Neil Diamond and Tammy Wynette. Eric Clapton and his band Derek and the Dominos visited the Ryman. Creedence Clearwater Revival came aboard, and so did the immortal Louis Armstrong. John joined in often, pairing with Armstrong on "Blue Yodel No. 9" and with Dylan on "Girl from the North Country." He and Carl Perkins teamed with Clapton and his mates on Perkins's "Matchbox," which had been introduced to much of the American audience via the Beatles' cover. In this picture, we see two brethren in arms—yesterday, today and for years to come. Waylon Jennings and John had been fellow travelers, even roommates, in the 1960s (a combustible concept). Here, Waylon, trying to jump-start a solo career that wouldn't really turn over for a few more years, gets an assist from the star on a medley of his own "Only Daddy That'll Walk The Line," John's "The Singing Star's Queen" and Chuck Berry's "Brown Eyed Handsome Man." As we will learn later in these pages, these two fast friends would continue to circle around each other, collaborating as musicians, being there when a strong shoulder was needed. "Waylon and Willie" became twinned in the 1970s when the so-called outlaw movement came riding out of Texas to dominate the country music scene, but Waylon and John were equally close—and, when you look at each man's heritage in rockabilly, in some ways closer.

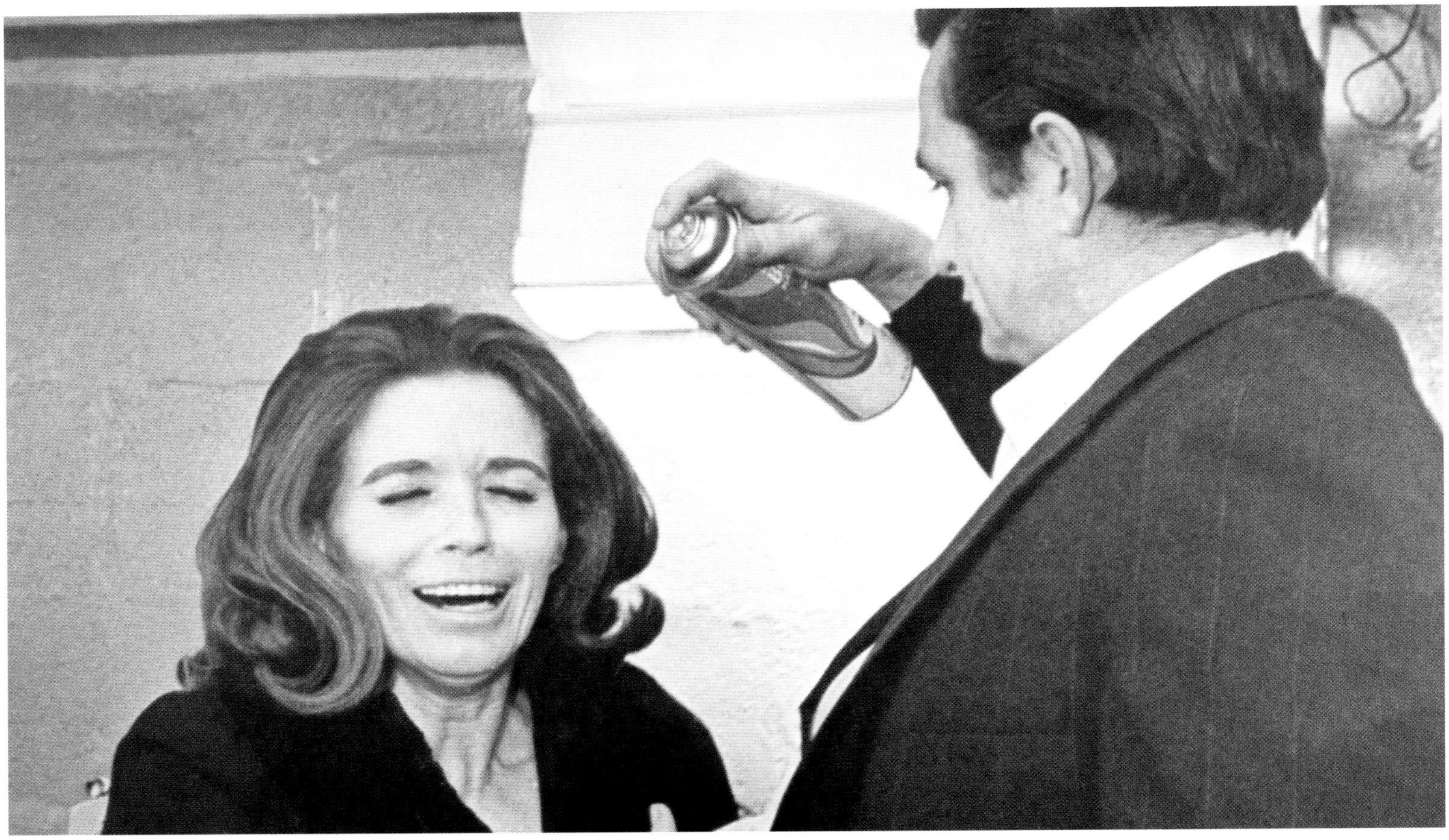

J.T. PHILLIPS (4)

A CONSTANT STAR on John's show, and now the guiding star in his life, was June, seen here and on the next two pages, goofing and performing with her husband. They dueted for the TV audience on not only "Jackson" but also such numbers as "Turn Around" and "'Cause I Love You." June reprised her earliest hit, a No. 9 country single in 1949. Any guesses? It was a rendition of the Christmas-season chestnut "Baby, It's Cold Outside," which is often done sexy but not when it's being sung by one of the wholesomer-than-thou Carter Family girls alongside the country/comic duo Homer and Jethro. June's devoutness influenced John; the new Johnny Cash, a proud Christian, wouldn't shy from his faith on the air, despite the skittishness of ABC execs. Then again, he adamantly refused their suggestion that he cut the word *stoned* from his performance of Kris Kristofferson's "Sunday Mornin' Comin' Down." So maybe he was ecumenical after all—or just a stubborn cuss whenever the suits tried to tell him what to do.

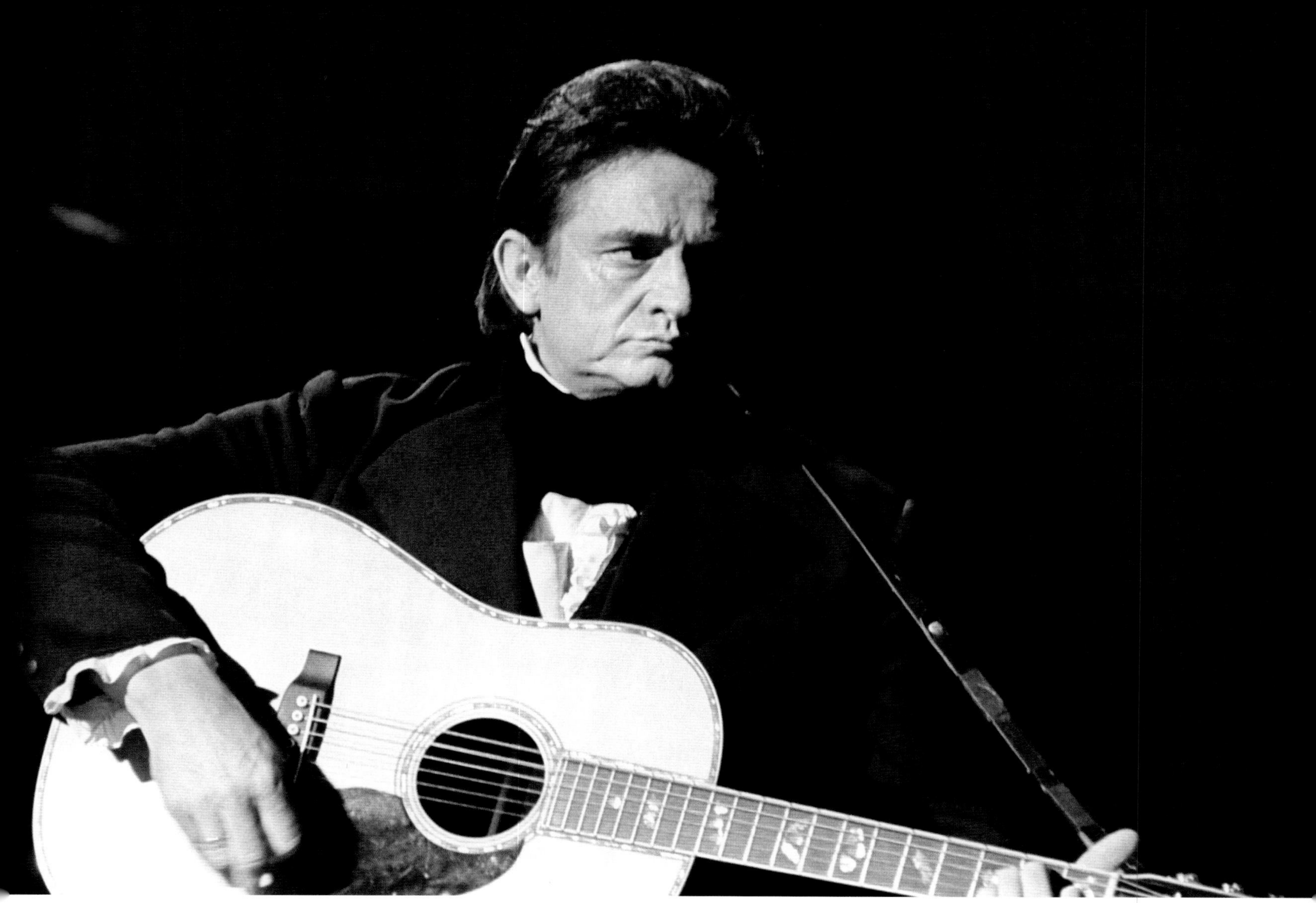

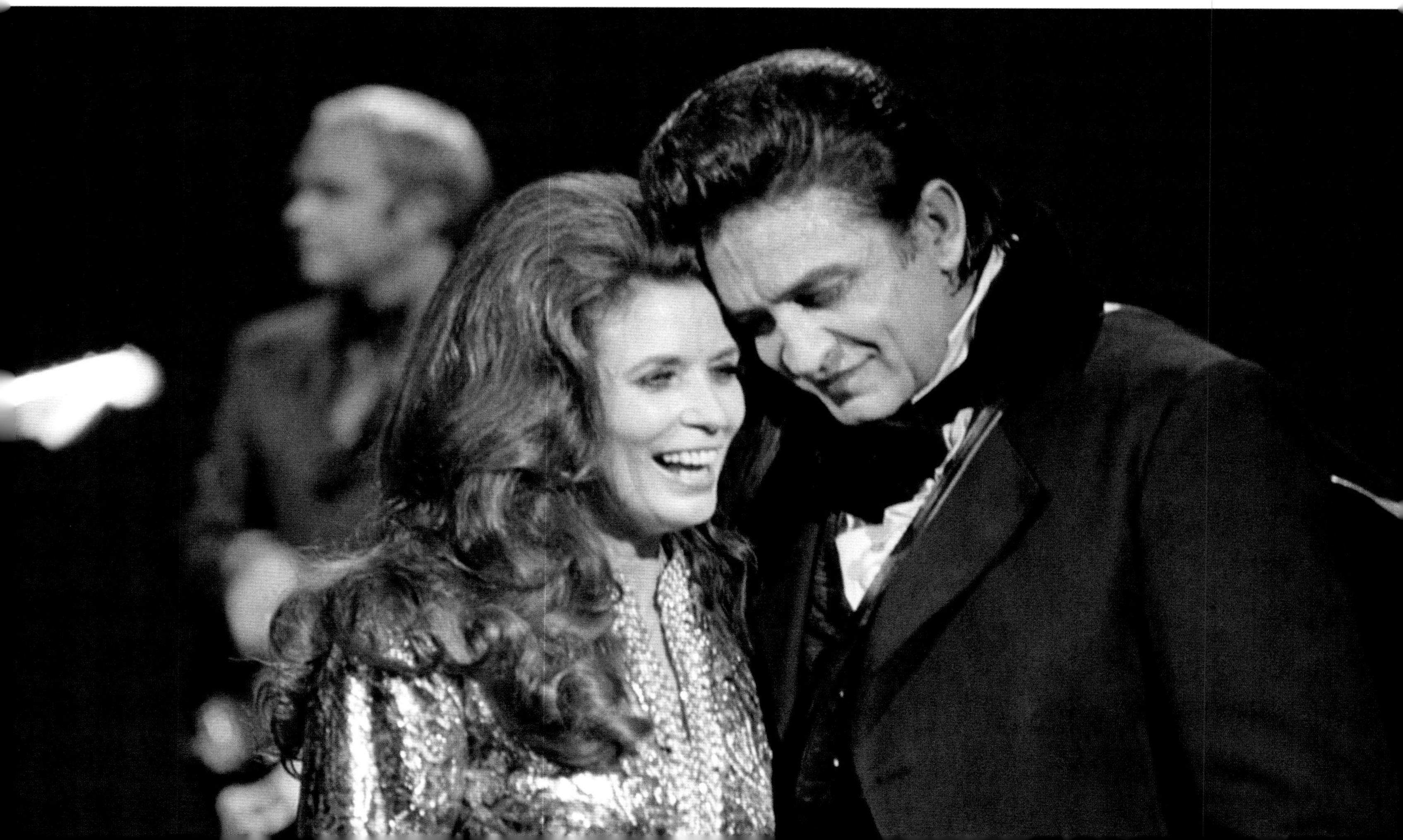

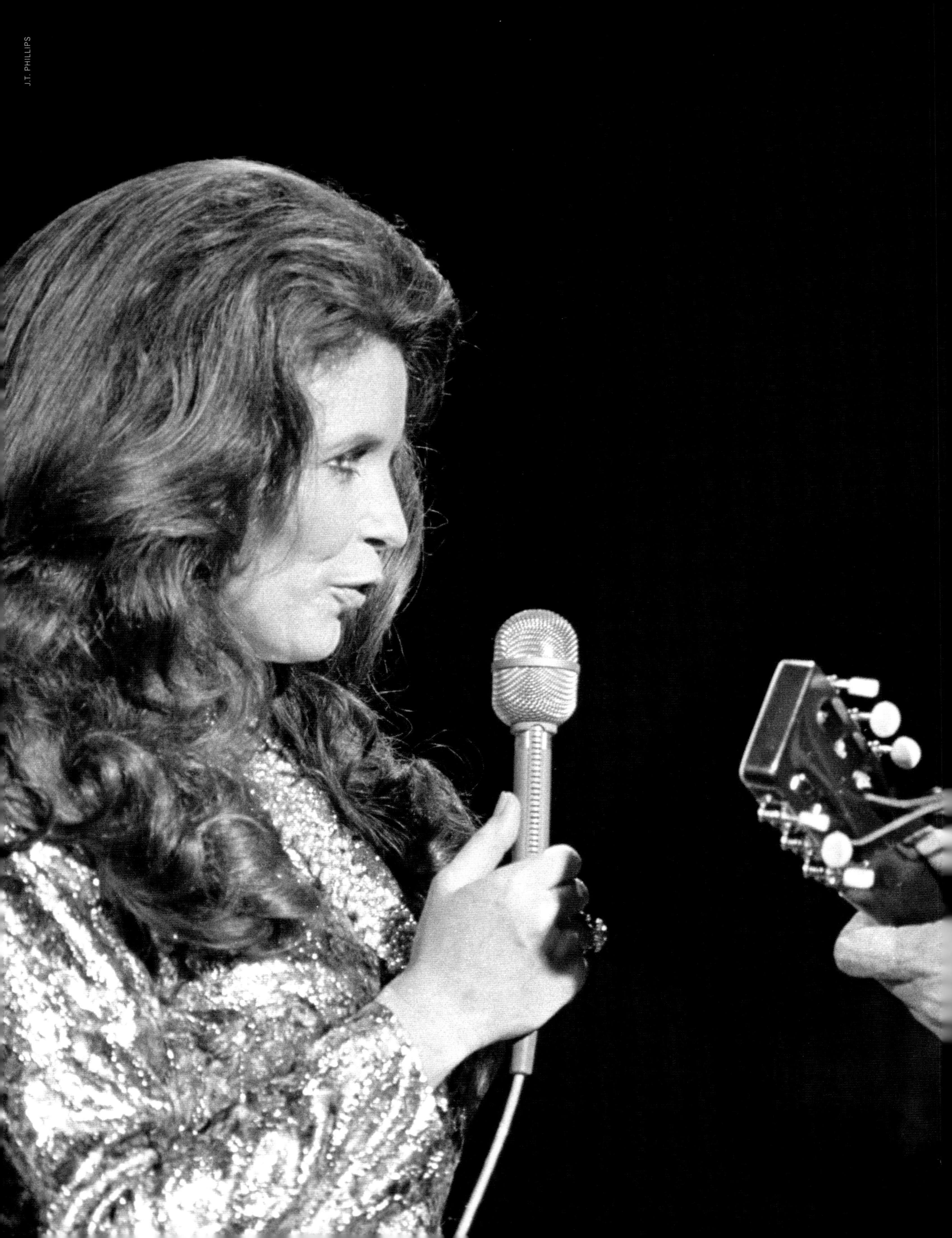

J.T. PHILLIPS

J.T. PHILLIPS (3)

FOR THE FINALE of *The Johnny Cash Show*'s second season in 1970, John was onstage with a mature woman and started to tell a story in that from-the-pulpit way of his. He reminisced about the first song he had ever sung in public, "when I was 12 years old, back at a little church in Dyess, Arkansas." The song was "The Unclouded Day," and he planned to do this hymn again on this night, for the folks watching at home. "And here's the lady that accompanied me on that song, my mother." Carrie and the son she had named J.R. 38 years earlier then performed beautifully and simply. John gave his mother a kiss and said, "Momma, that was fine." The year after he died, a collection of gospel songs by John, all of which had been taught to him by Carrie, was released under the accurate title *My Mother's Hymn Book.* He had recorded those 15 songs when old and frail, and he said in the liner notes that this was the favorite of all of his many, many albums.

AGAIN, CARRIE is at the keyboard and again it is 1970: Here and on the next four pages, a gathering of the Cash clan for Ray and Carrie's 50th wedding anniversary celebration. In this picture, John's father, Ray, is looking on from the end of the piano, and several of John's siblings surround. Sister Louise, now Mrs. Joe Garrett is at near left, and then there's sister Reba (Mrs. Don Hancock) and brother Roy. On either side of Ray are sister Joanne (then Mrs. Billy Ingle; now Joanne Cash Yates) and brother Tommy, and then John himself. On the following page, clockwise from top: Grandkids Kelly Hancock, Jeff Ingle, Mark Cash and Tara Cash steal the show; then the middle generation gathers, with Joanne, Louise, Reba (in front) and Tommy, John and Roy; and finally, in a mix of those two generations, John holds John Carter Cash as John's eldest daughter, Rosanne, looks on happily. On the page after that, the celebrants cut the cake. These folks have come a long way from Dyess to a fantastic lakeside spread in Tennessee, but they're still the same people.

J.T. PHILLIPS

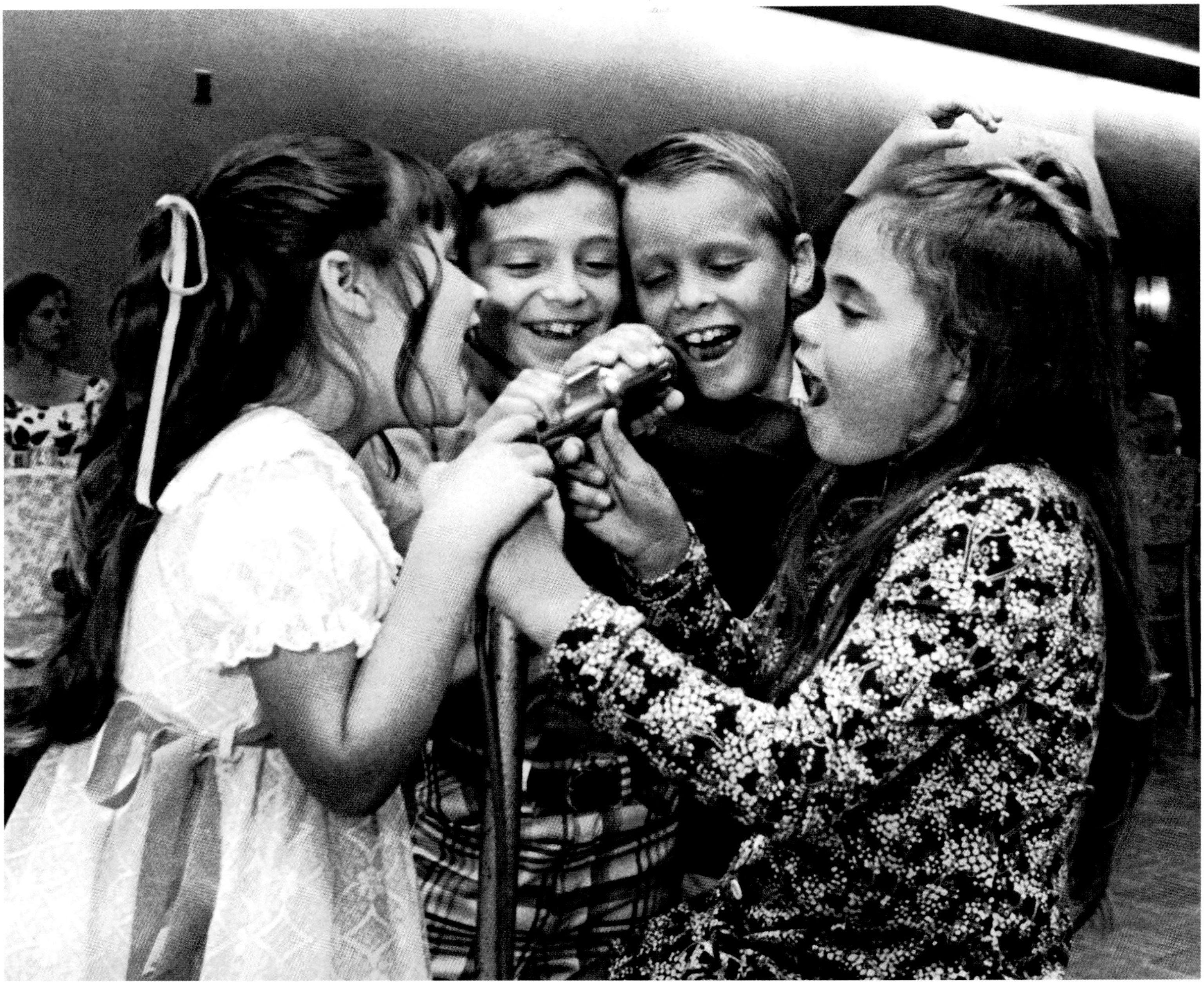

IN THE CENTER is the happy couple after a half century of marriage: Ray and Carrie Cash. Behind them are, from left, Gloria Cash, Carlene Smith (known as the country singer Carlene Carter), Reba Hancock, Louise Garrett, Roy Cash, Tommy Cash, Joanne Ingle, John and John Carter Cash, Rosanne Cash, Kathy Cash and Ricky Hancock, Don and Reba's son. The kids in front are, from left, back row: Rhonda Ingle (Joanne's daughter), Mark Cash (Tommy's son), and Jeff Ingle (Joanne's son). Second row, from left: Paula Cash (Tommy's daughter), Tara Cash (Johnny's daughter), Charlotte Ingle (Joanne's daughter), Cindy Cash (Johnny's daughter), Timmy Hancock (Reba's son), and Paul Brent Garrett (Louise's son). Lastly, the three young ladies in the front row, from left: Darla Cash (Roy's daughter), Kelly Hancock (Reba's daughter), and Rosie Nix (June's daughter). Certainly much of the conversation during this celebratory gathering is about Carrie and Ray and the progress of—and burgeoning of—the Cash family. Certainly, too, a lot of it is about the glory John had conferred on the clan through the years: a big singing star, and now a major TV star, too. Everyone in this photo is, at the moment, riding high.

OUTLAW OR EMINENCE?

THIS IS AN OUTTAKE from the cover shoot for the album *Heroes* by Johnny Cash and Waylon Jennings. Johnny was not considered one of the country music "outlaws"—the Waylon, Willie Nelson, Jerry Jeff Walker gang that might today be called alt-country but at the time was called outlaw—who giddyapped the charts in the 1970s. But he was, to these new stars, a father figure. He had been there, done that; they loved his music, they loved him. John was still keeping on in this period, and making some great music—but fewer folks seemed to notice.

SHOOTING BLANKS is what John is up to during a photo shoot for his 1977 Columbia album *The Last Gunfighter Ballad,* and—as a metaphor—it's what he was up to commercially for much of the 1970s and '80s. (This album reached a high of No. 29 on the country charts, and its best-selling single reached No. 38.) Personally, John was going through changes in this period and trying to help in raising the family. His association with the Highwaymen aside—and we'll get to that later in our book—these were years that are largely forgotten by his casual fans. They know about Sun Studio, perhaps, and the 1960s hits and the TV show (which ended its meteoric run in 1971 when ABC, like other networks, cut most of their "adult" fare and catered more to the youth audience; even Lawrence Welk, after 16 years on ABC, got the boot). These Johnny Cash fans know about that earlier stuff, and they're well aware of the American Recordings renaissance nearer the end of his life. But what was Johnny Cash up to in the '70s and '80s, anyway?

He was hunkering down, concentrating on faith and family, trying at intervals to get or stay clean and sober, making some music (but even here: His association with Columbia, which looked like it might last forever, ended in 1986), recording those wonderful, spare gospel songs in his home studio in Hendersonville, and basically hanging on. Born again as a Christian with June's influence in the late '60s, he determined then to quit amphetamines. That effort took two years, but by most accounts, when John Carter Cash was born in 1970, John, thinking of his new son, kicked uppers. There was backsliding, then, and a stint at the Betty Ford Center in California, in 1983. (On YouTube, there's an inspiring clip of John and Waylon Jennings together on David Letterman's show in the 1980s, each man talking—with good humor and some quiet pride—about being clean after decades-long addictions.) There would be another relapse and another period in rehab in Nashville in 1992, then a third stint in a different California facility in 1992. So sobriety was a near-constant battle, as any addict knows, and this would all become part of the story when Johnny Cash ascended again—returning front and center to the public consciousness, meantime developing an entirely new and much younger fan base—in the mid-1990s.

According to John Carter Cash's book and other memoirs, there were times of financial and marital strife as well, but his parents ultimately persevered. Meantime, Johnny's children and their cousins grew and married, and the number of Cash or Carter grandchildren visiting at the lake house swelled to enormous proportions. This last part was all good.

Eminence or outlaw? John would have demurred, saying he was neither and never had been. But he picked up the lifetime achievement awards when they were proffered and kept singing songs the only way he knew how. We are fortunate that he was in a profession where work is preserved. A true joy in recent years has been discovering or rediscovering the music Johnny Cash made when it seemed he had gone away.

BILL BARNES

J.T. PHILLIPS

WEDDINGS AND WAKES

are part of getting older: marrying off the kids, bidding farewell to old friends. Rebecca Carlene Smith, June's daughter better known as the country singer Carlene Carter, got an early start in marriage when, in 1971, only 16 years old, she wed Joe Simpkins. That union lasted till 1972 and produced a daughter; Carlene would marry thrice more and have one more child, a son. From 1979 to 1990 her husband was the British singer Nick Lowe, one example of the Carter-Cash clan's propensity to wed within the industry. Rosanne Cash was married from 1979 to 1992 to the country singer Rodney Crowell; Rosanne's sister Cindy was married to Marty Stuart from 1983 to 1988, and there have been other workplace liaisons—including Carlene's longtime romance with bassist Howie Epstein of Tom Petty and the Heartbreakers. That association leads to another topic that has affected the next generation of the family: the temptations of the music business. Carlene started singing with her mother and aunts in the Carter Sisters, then had enormous personal success with the hit country album *I Fell in Love,* the title track of which was a No. 3 single. Epstein produced that album and co-wrote that song. In 2001, though, the roller-coaster ride was different: He and Carlene were busted for drug possession in New Mexico, and a year and a half later he was dead of a suspected overdose. Carlene Carter has survived, although her career faded. Only a few years ago she played a solo set at a park in Long Island, New York, during which she teared up while singing a song dedicated to her late younger sister, the singer Rosie Nix Adams, who had died at age 45 in 2003—the same year John and June passed. Weddings and wakes: They mark the passage of lives being lived. On the following pages, it's all happiness in more family photos from Carlene's big day in 1971, clockwise from left: John, June, John Carter and the bride; the newlyweds exiting the church; cutting the cake.

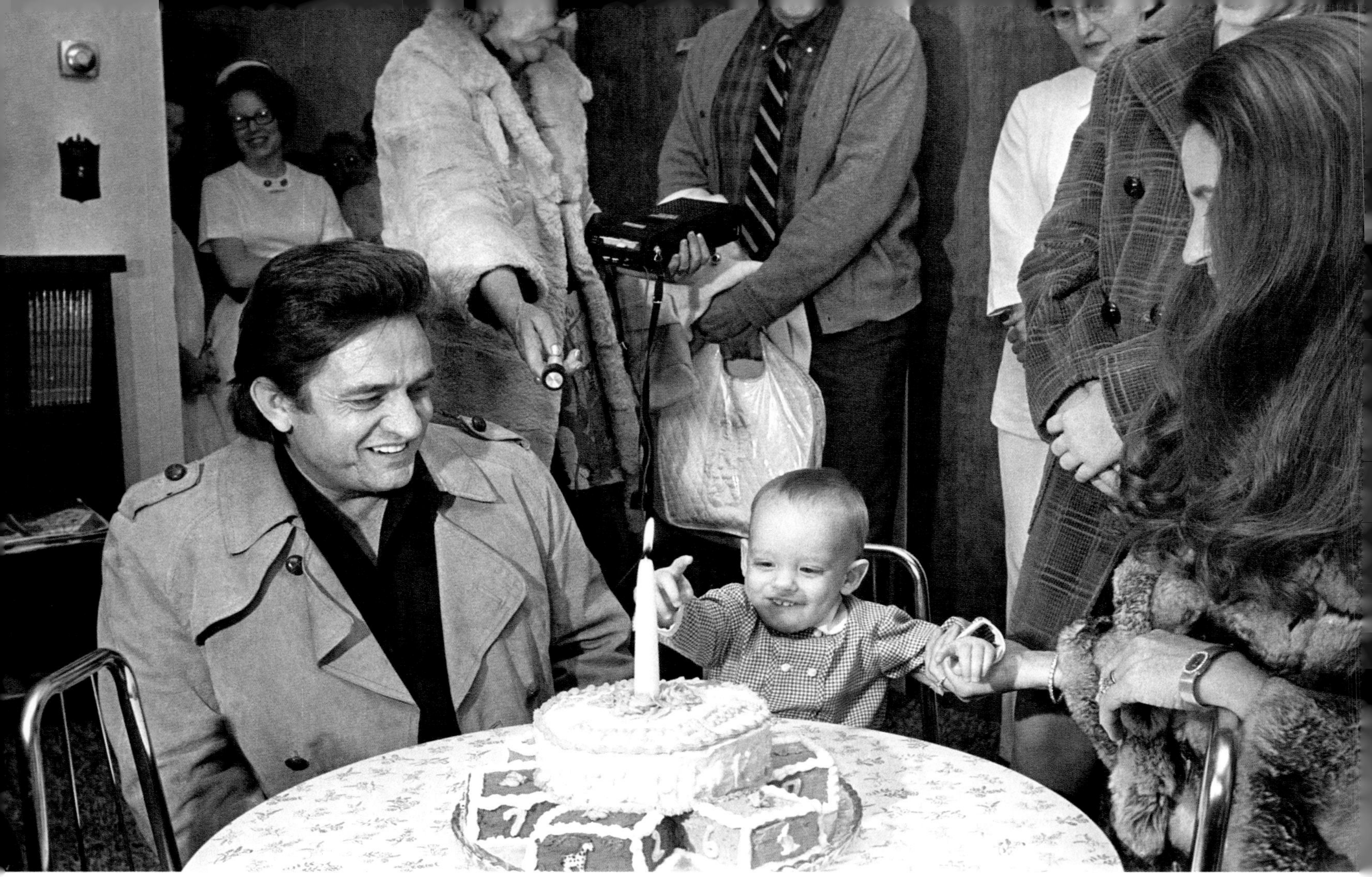

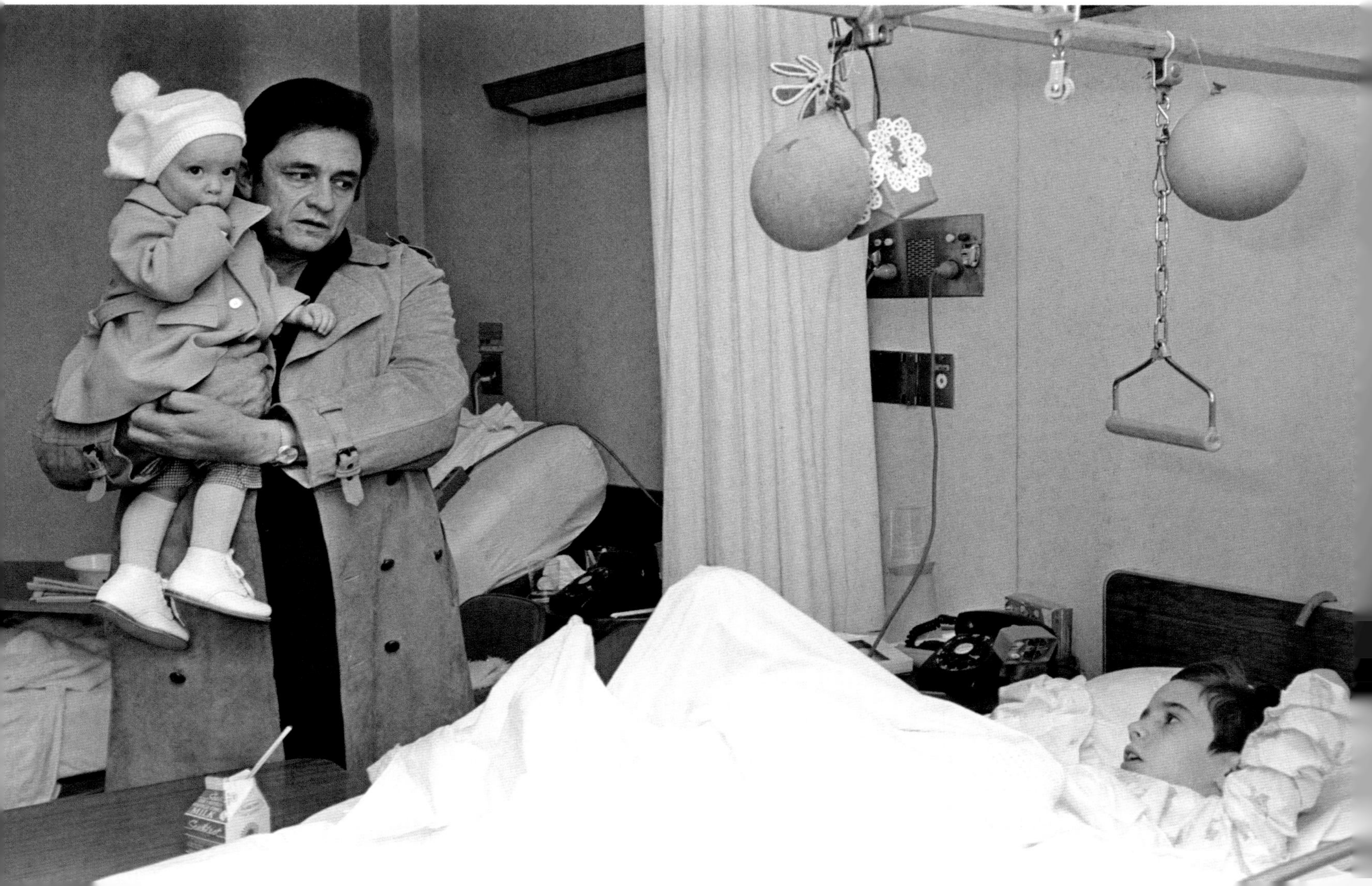
MILK

COURTESY HOUSE OF CASH

JOHN CARTER CASH, who turns one and celebrates on the opposite page at the Nashville hospital where he was born, leaving behind a plaque that reads "Donated to Madison Hospital by John Carter Cash February 1971." In the photograph at bottom, father (who really made the donation) and son visit a young patient. Above, a few years later, the family about to travel in a fashion befitting modern American singing stars. John Carter tells LIFE a funny story today: "I came into the world at the height of my parents' careers. They did not slow down their touring when I came along but simply took me with them. Not long ago I met a man who had been on a plane with my parents early in 1971, and he told me he had said to my mother, 'So you bring your little one on the road with you?' And my mother answered, 'He's already got 750,000 frequent flyer miles!'"

WARREN COUNTY
473-8444
PUTNAM COUNTY
526-2181

BEDFORD COUNTY
684-6611
OR
684-6612

SUMNER COUNTY
GALLATIN
452-0404
MARSHALL COUNTY
-3555

MAU
C
388
MT.
379

HICKMA
729-

TROUSDA
374-

J.T. PHILLIPS

JOHN'S SENSE of empathy was deep, and through the years he was always giving back—even when his own bank account was dwindling. He supported, among other things and causes, children's orphanages, mental-health associations, homes for autistic kids, refuges for battered women, prisoner's rights groups, Native American rights advocacy organizations, the Nashville Symphony, a burn research center, the American Cancer Society, the YWCA, Youth for Christ, Campus Life (another teen support group) and humane societies for animals. Here and on the next two pages, he serves as the honorary chairperson of a local telethon in Nashville that, in 1970, is raising money to battle cerebral palsy. His name and face were particularly invaluable to charities in this period because of the television show, and John spread himself thin, thankful for what he and his family had been given.

GOODNESS KNOWS from here on in—from the 1970s through to 2003—John was given many awards, particularly from various music organizations and halls of fame—but surely among those that meant the most to him were the Anti-Defamation League's Americanism Award, the Youth for Christ's Man of the Year award, the Audie Murphy Patriotism Award, the Shalom Peace Award and the first ever First Amendment Center/Americana Music Association "Spirit of Americana" Free Speech Award. Just by the way, in 1991 he also won the Angel Award for *The Spoken Word,* his reading of the New Testament on audio tape.

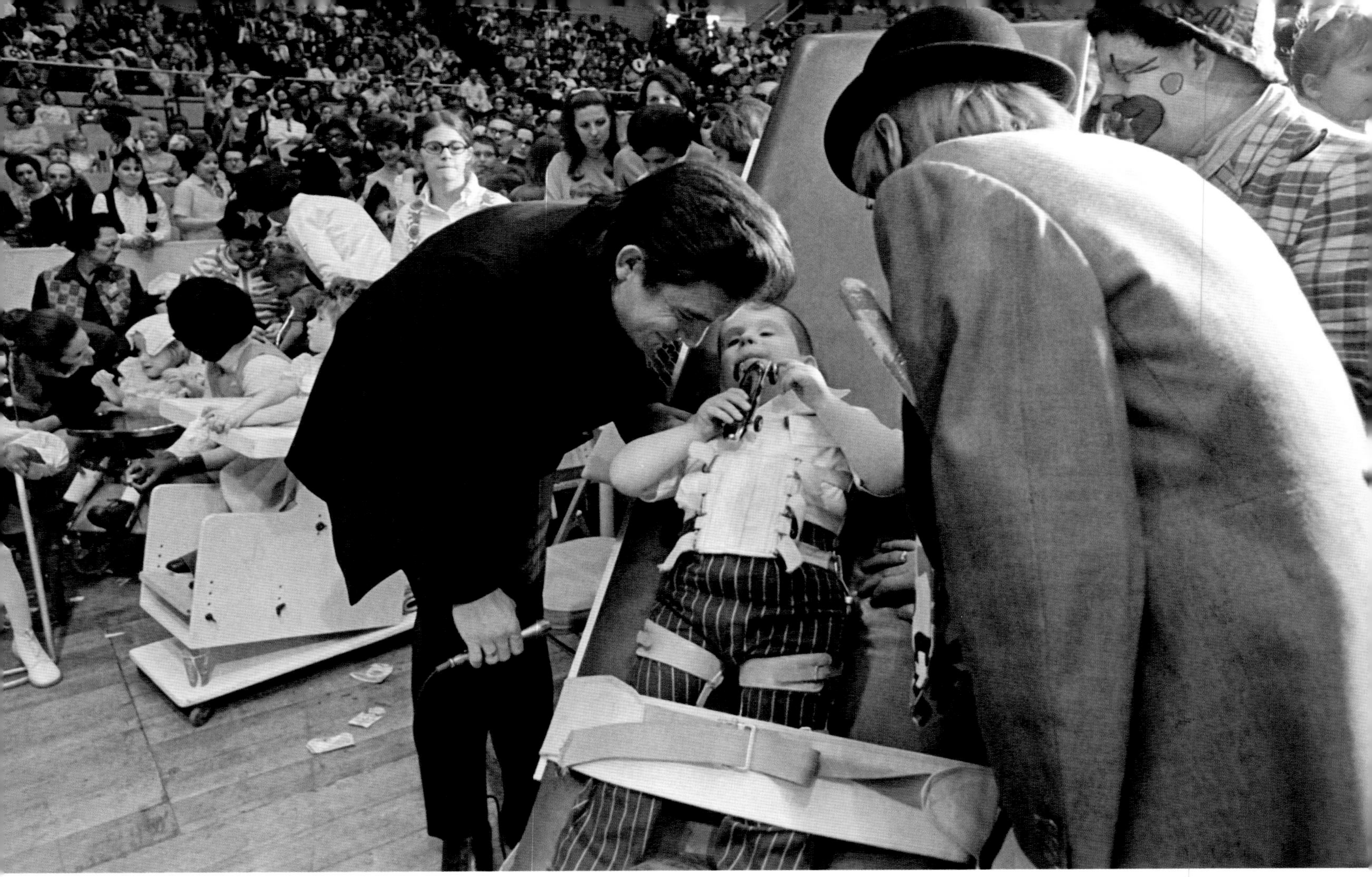

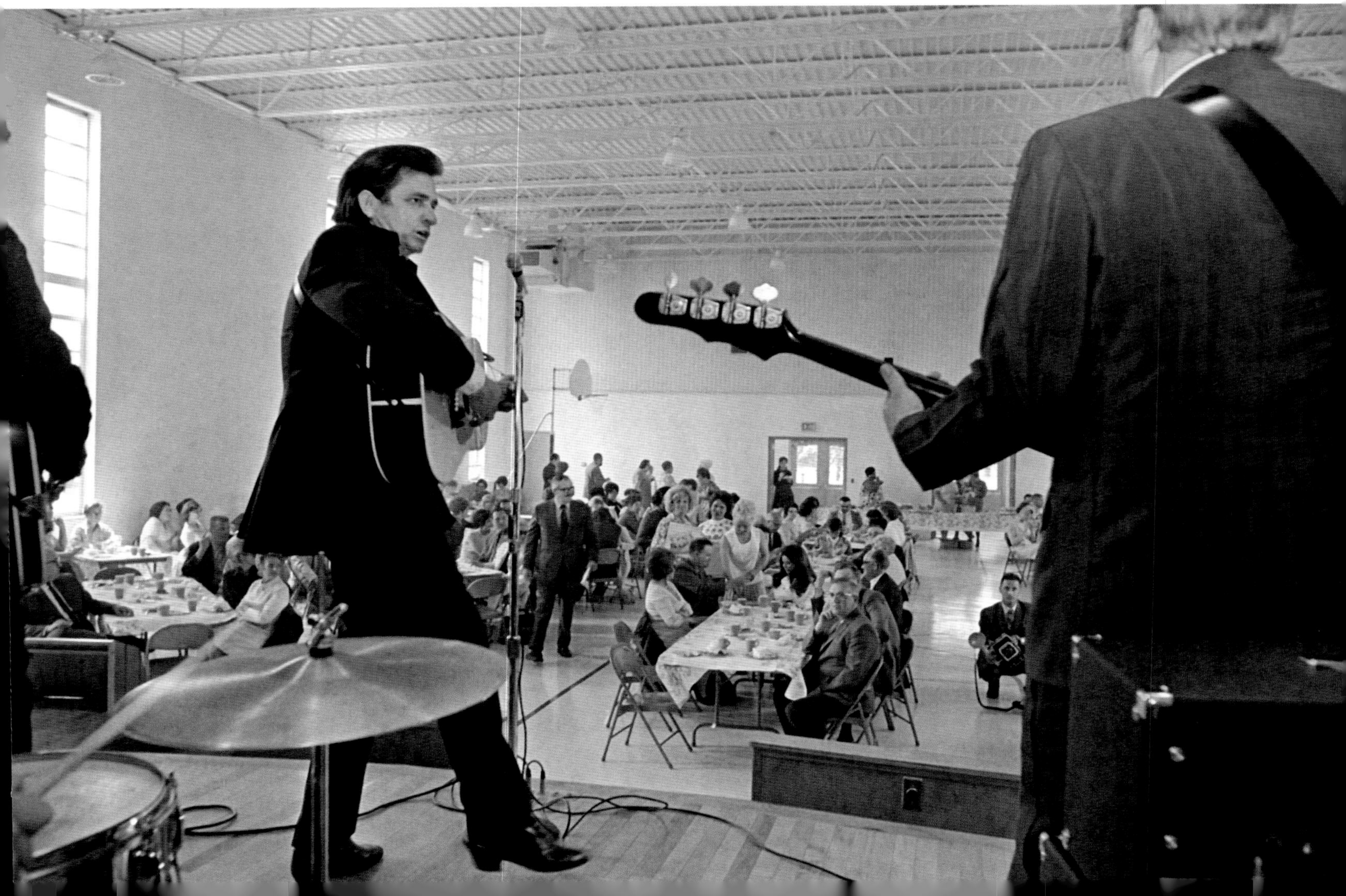

J.T. PHILLIPS

A SYMBOLIC READING

of this photograph could be that in the 1970s and '80s, Johnny Cash was forced to take his act from the airplane to the bus. But that reading would be unfair. He remained a major star, even if his records, besides the greatest hits and other "catalogue" packages, were no longer selling. After 1971, he would crack the U.S. Top 100 pop singles chart only twice more during his career (with "Kate" reaching No. 75 in 1972 and "One Piece at a Time" reaching No. 29 in 1976) and would not return to the fore of the cultural conversation until his partnership in the Highwaymen and then, more, with his American Recordings. Nevertheless, it should be said: Country stars do like buses, often preferring them to planes. John's great friend Willie Nelson has said that the Internal Revenue Service (the "Infernal Revenue Service") did him an inadvertent favor by busting him for back taxes and making him give up, among other things, his jet. He found he liked life better back on the bus anyway, and he still travels to more than 100 gigs a year that way—at age 80.

DON HUNSTEIN (3)

HARMONY was always easily achieved by June and John when the microphones were on (seen here, working and taking cuddlesome breaks from work at the Columbia Recording Studio on 30th Street in New York City in July of 1975). Harmony at home was sometimes harder to come by, but they worked at it, they always worked at it. And in the end, they found what they required. It has been written than June was regularly worried that John might relapse or stray from their marriage. John, for his part, knew he was flawed—as are we all—and in his maturity desperately wanted to beat back his demons.

WINDBLOWN IN THE '70s,
on the page opposite, and at right: born
again. In this sequence of pictures,
Pastor John Cobaugh baptizes John in
the Jordan River in 1979. The two most
important things during his homeward
trek were his wife and his faith. He
blended them when he and June were
the first to record songwriter Terry
Smith's "Far Side Banks of Jordan,"
which has become a modern gospel
classic, covered more than 150 times.
The Cashes revisited the song for June's
1999 solo comeback album, *Press On,*
which was produced by their son,
John Carter Cash, and which won a
Grammy. The lyrics in part: "But if
it proves to be His will that I am the first
to cross / And somehow I've a feeling
it will be / When it comes your time to
travel likewise don't feel lost / For I
will be the first one that you'll see / And
I'll be waiting on the far side banks of
Jordan . . ." The Reverend Billy Graham
said when John died: "[He] was a
close personal friend. Johnny was a
good man who also struggled with
many challenges in his life."

IN THIS LAST CHAPTER,
John takes a look back, and at one point in the past, LIFE prompted him, asking the question: "What singers do you particularly admire?" We weren't looking for "Trent Reznor" or "Bono," but in any event John answered, "Hank Snow is my favorite. I just bought his boxed set last month. I was with Rick Rubin, my new producer. We went to Tower Records, and I saw it and said, 'Did you ever listen to Hank Snow?' And he said, 'No, I don't think I've ever heard of him.' I said, 'Well, you're going to.' I bought it, we took it to his house, and Rick kept it." This was John's last campaign: listening to what he wanted to, telling the world why it was great, singing and playing a lot of it, and preparing for the future.

THE LEGEND
LIVES ON

THE HIGHWAYMEN were not a supergroup by any means when they first got together in 1985; they were four good friends hanging out, and billed as such—"Waylon Jennings, Willie Nelson, Johnny Cash, Kris Kristofferson"—on that first album, which was called *Highwayman* after a Jimmy Webb tune, which in this version happened to go to No. 1 on the U.S. country singles chart, as did the LP on the album chart, which meant these guys needed a name, which meant they were the Highwaymen. By the time they recorded a sequel album five years later, this is how they were known, and for some members of this quartet, the sum of the parts equaled a better meal ticket than the solo career.

Maybe that's a harsh—which isn't to say inaccurate—appraisal of the facts. Any of these artists could, at any time, stand on his own. That was certainly true of John (though he admittedly hadn't seen the No. 1 spot on any commercial list for a while). If the question in our prior chapter was "outlaw or eminence?" by the mid-1980s the question had been emphatically answered: Here was the eminence, the link back to the Carter Family and Elvis and even Hank. Cash was the continuum, and he was still as unique and mesmeric, in his voice and charisma, as he had ever been.

By this point, John Carter Cash was hanging in the cabin studio and wherever else his mother or father might record, and he remembers to LIFE: "When Dad joined to make music with Willie, Kris and Waylon, the result was magic. What made this possible was the fact they were naturally at ease with each other. Nothing was ever forced. They were as close as brothers."

Willie is to the fore in this picture, then (from left) we see John's head, Waylon on guitar and Kris in the back. Kris was the kid, and John remembered to LIFE in 1994 how they first connected: "Kris was a janitor at CBS. He used to slip tapes of his songs into my wife's purse. The next time he saw me he'd say, 'Did you hear that song?' I'd say, 'Not yet, but I will.' And this went on for a long time. In fact, I had so many tapes come in that I just didn't want to hear them. I used to open the balcony to our lakeside home and throw them in the water. Then one Sunday afternoon he landed a helicopter out in my yard. He landed a helicopter, fell out with a beer in one hand and a tape in the other and said, 'You're gonna listen to my song.' I said, 'Come on in.' I listened to 'Sunday Mornin' Comin' Down.' I listened to all of his songs after that."

WAYLON, WILLIE, KRIS AND JOHNNY
represented, for some fans, the greatest generation of postwar country music singers, songwriters and stars. Whether they were coming together as the Highwaymen in the mid-'80s to the mid-'90s, or cracking up as John and Willie are doing at top while trying to smile politely, they'd earned the fancy backdrop and the kind lighting. There was no hiding the wrinkles at this point, or the wars waged through the years. But—almost weirdly—these four were back on top, in advance of Garth Brooks, Travis Tritt and all who would follow. "You know," John told LIFE late in this period, "I miss the tried-and-true and the dyed-in-the-wool. I guess that's a typical comment from an artist my age. Glory for the new artists, great. But country radio doesn't program hardly anybody over 40. Country music is about tradition. And they're losing that tradition, in my mind, anyway."

ALAN MESSER (2)

JIM MCGUIRE

WALTER R. KIENLE

HOMEWARD BOUND is what John was when he reunited with Jerry Lee Lewis and Carl Perkins (left) in 1981 at an impromptu concert in Stuttgart, West Germany. LIFE asked him, in 1994, for his recollection of those so-long-ago Sun sessions, and he answered acutely about Sam Phillips, while repeating much of his favorite story, and a few of his favorite lines: "He didn't discover me. I called him three times and was turned down. Finally, I just sat on his steps one morning and waited with my guitar beside me. He came up, and evidently he'd had a good night. So I said, 'I'm Johnny Cash, I think if you'd listen to me that you'd be glad you did.' That line has never failed me. He said, 'Well, come on in, let's hear it.' The first thing I recorded with Sam was 'Wide Open Road' and then 'Folsom Prison Blues.' But he liked 'Hey, Porter' better, and he said, 'Go home and write me a weeper to go with it, a crying-in-your-beer song.' So I went home and wrote 'Cry, Cry, Cry.' I thought that really sounded like a weeper—not cry once, but cry three times. You know, Sam had a vision. We need more of that today." On the following pages: more of what we need today, Willie Nelson and Johnny Cash, in 1998.

THE WORD "RENAISSANCE" is—as we said about *treasure trove* back in our introduction—overused in the press. It is trotted out to describe a moderately successful comeback single or movie, or someone getting back to work after rehab. But there is, or can be or should be, a spiritual connotation to the word, and certainly before he died John enjoyed what was called—everywhere, by everyone—his final renaissance. He told LIFE how he came in touch with Rick Rubin, the producer who believed in him: "He heard I wanted to cut ties with Mercury Records because it had been an unsuccessful venture, on their part and my part. So Rick called my manager and said he'd like to sign me. He didn't say he'd like to talk about it, he said he'd like to sign me. So when we met, I asked him, 'What kind of album would you like me to record?' And he said, 'Whatever Johnny Cash is, that's what I want on a record.' He made me feel like Sam Phillips made me feel." Yes, indeed: Some of life's journeys were coming around again. Many of the songs were old songs, and some of the new ones that John would come to own were done in new ways, which were old ways at heart. There would be four—or IV—American Recordings released while John was alive, II more posthumously, plus the box set *Unearthed.* The pictures on this page are outtakes from the photo sessions for his first Rick Rubin–produced album, *American Recordings.* The concept was merely conceptual—John wasn't throwing away the guitar or walking away from the music, not quite yet.

JOHN'S LAST ALBUM while he was alive was *American IV: The Man Comes Around;* the portrait here in the field and the one at the end of our book were made for the *Unchained* CD. He was in great pain during his final years; to return to the testimony of Rosanne Cash that began our book: "He was so sick [and] the music really kept him alive—his final burst of genius." Perhaps the most well-known images of this period are from the memorable video of "Hurt," Johnny Cash's cover version of the song by Trent Reznor's Nine Inch Nails, on *The Man Comes Around.* Some have seen this short film as his epitaph, but that seems too easy. His last acts—not on film—were his epitaph. John was ill before June died, and quickly became sicker. So many previous chroniclers have said—and in this, they're not wrong—that it was altogether fitting and even poetic that June and John chased one another to heaven. In July of 2003, two months before his death, John performed one last time, at the Carter Family Fold, near Bristol, Tennessee, saying before he sang, "The spirit of June Carter overshadows me tonight with the love she had for me and the love I have for her. We connect somewhere between here and heaven. She came down for a short visit, I guess, from heaven to visit with me tonight to give me courage and inspiration like she always has."

It has been 10 years now that we've been without them, John and June. Their family was graced by their presence in this temporal realm, to be sure, and so were we, all of the fans of John and June and Vivian and Rosanne and John Carter and Maybelle and Tommy and Roy and Ray and Jack and Tara and . . . well, we needn't go on; the point is made: all of the fans of all of the Cashes and Carters—this remarkable American family that has reached out through the many years and touched us all.

ANDREW EARL